Here Am I, Lord . . .
Send Somebody
Else

Here Am I, Lord . . . Send Somebody Else

How God Uses Ordinary People To Do Extraordinary Things

JILL BRISCOE

W PUBLISHING GROUP

AN IMPRINT OF THOMAS NELSON

Published in Nashville, Tennessee, by W Publishing, an imprint of Thomas Nelson.

Thomas Nelson titles may be purchased in bulk for educational, business, fund-raising, or sales promotional use. For information, please e-mail SpecialMarkets@ThomasNelson.com.

Any Internet addresses, phone numbers, or company or product information printed in this book are offered as a resource and are not intended in any way to be or to imply an endorsement by Thomas Nelson, nor does Thomas Nelson vouch for the existence, content, or services of these sites, phone numbers, companies, or products beyond the life of this book.

Unless otherwise noted, Scripture quotations are taken from the Holy Bible, New International Version®, NIV®. Copyright © 1973, 1978, 1984, 2011 by Biblica, Inc.™ Used by permission of Zondervan. All rights reserved worldwide. www.zondervan.com. The "NIV" and "New International Version" are trademarks registered in the United States Patent and Trademark Office by Biblica, Inc.™

Scripture quotations marked KJV are from the King James Version, public domain.

Scripture quotations marked ESV are from the ESV® Bible (The Holy Bible, English Standard Version®). Copyright © 2001 by Crossway, a publishing ministry of Good News Publishers. Used by permission. All rights reserved.

Scripture quotations marked THE MESSAGE are from The Message. Copyright © by Eugene H. Peterson 1993, 1994, 1995, 1996, 2000, 2001, 2002. Used by permission of NavPress. All rights reserved. Represented by Tyndale House Publishers, Inc.

Scripture quotations marked NASB are from the New American Standard Bible®. Copyright © 1960, 1962, 1963, 1968, 1971, 1972, 1973, 1975, 1977, 1995 by The Lockman Foundation. Used by permission. (www.Lockman.org)

Scripture quotations marked NKJV are from the New King James Version®. Copyright © 1982 by Thomas Nelson. Used by permission. All rights reserved.

Scripture quotations marked NLT are from the Holy Bible, New Living Translation. © 1996, 2004, 2007, 2013, 2015 by Tyndale House Foundation. Used by permission of Tyndale House Publishers, Inc., Carol Stream, Illinois 60188. All rights reserved.

Scripture quotations marked PHILLIPS are from The New Testament in Modern English, Revised Edition. © J. B. Phillips 1958, 1960, 1972. Used by permission of Macmillan Publishing Co., Inc.

Scripture quotations marked RSV are from the Revised Standard Version of the Bible. Copyright 1946, 1952, and 1971 National Council of the Churches of Christ in the United States of America. Used by permission. All rights reserved.

Scripture quotations marked TLB are from The Living Bible. Copyright © 1971. Used by permission of Tyndale House Publishers, Inc., Carol Stream, Illinois 60188. All rights reserved.

ISBN 978-0-7852-1676-6 (eBook)
ISBN 978-0-7852-1678-0 (TP)

Library of Congress Cataloging-in-Publication Data

The Library of Congress has catalogued the earlier edition as follows:
Briscoe, Jill.
    Here am I, Lord—send somebody else / by Jill Briscoe.
    p. cm.
    Includes bibliographical references.
    ISBN 0-8499-4445-7 (softcover)
    1. Fear—Religious aspects—Christianity. 2. Christian life. I. Title.
BV4908.5.B74 2004
    248.4—dc22   2004001652

Printed in the United States of America

18 19 20 21 22 LSC 10 9 8 7 6 5 4 3 2 1

To our children, David, Judy, and Pete, who have
all been sweetly obedient to the call of God

CONTENTS

ACKNOWLEDGMENTS

I am indebted to many people for shepherding this book from concept to the printed page, but especially want to thank Debbie Wickwire and Laura Kendall at W Publishing Group for their attention to every detail, large and small; Jennifer Stair for her sharp editorial eye; and Alive Communications, our agents and friends.

And now I trust that this new edition, all these years later, will be an encouragement to the next generation for them to listen and respond to the call of God.

NOTE FROM THE AUTHOR

This book contains lessons learned from the first five books of Moses. Readers would greatly benefit by familiarizing themselves with the narrative in the books of Genesis, Exodus, Leviticus, Numbers, and Deuteronomy.

FOREWORD

I first met Jill while visiting a maximum security prison in Texas. We bonded over a passion for Jesus and a love for women, no matter their age, background, or struggles. I knew the first time I met her that I'd found a hero in the faith. It was notable because I was craving heroes.

I think we all are.

A few years prior, at the beginning of my all-in desire to follow God, life was simpler, and I hadn't encountered much suffering. Ministry looked fun, and it was easy to dream about pouring out my life for God. But suffering found me and the people nearest to me, as it does everyone sooner or later. Ministry became less rewarding and involved more disappointment than reward.

And then came Jill.

The way she speaks about suffering and following Jesus is backward from everything I used to believe. She wants Jesus more than comfort, more than recognition or approval. And because of that deep love and passion for Him, suffering is a welcome friend who causes her to experience more of Him. Jill has taught me to embrace the things I might otherwise want to push away in my life, because those might be the very things that bring me more of Jesus.

After meeting Jill I invited her to speak at the IF:Gathering in 2017. The story she has told me now about that weekend in February is a perfect picture of the woman who wrote this book. Her retelling was this: she thought she was speaking at a youth rally of a few thousand teenagers, all eagerly waiting to hear from her that day—when in reality, her words echoed across 122 countries and in the ears of hundreds of thousands of people live across the world.

When she tells that story, her blue eyes sparkle and she laughs, because it doesn't matter to Jill how many people were in the room that day. She loved teaching the Word of God, reminding them that Jesus is better, and telling her stories of a life lived in service to Christ.

As her words burst into every corner of the Internet that day, I knew something special was happening. But it seems everyone else did, too, because as Jill walked off the stage, the entire room erupted in a standing ovation. I wasn't the only one who needed a hero in the faith—a generation of women were craving the same thing.

I believe we are in dire need of some humans to follow on this earth who have desperately and wholly sought after Christ. Jill would be the last to tell you that she is a hero, or anything special at all, for that matter. And dare we ever make an idol out of another human, the Apostle Paul said, "Follow my example, as I follow the example of Christ" (1 Corinthians 11:1).

That is who Jill has become to so many of us, which is why it brings me great joy that a new generation will find the words of this book and, I hope, follow her example as she continues to follow Christ. That would be a generation sold out indeed! And who knows what could happen if women across the earth believed that Jesus was worth everything? That could change everything.

—Jennie Allen
Author of *Nothing to Prove*
Founder and visionary of the IF: Gathering

ONE

A MOSES MOMENT

It was the sixties, and my husband was trying to capture the attention of some lively British teenagers during a wild youth meeting.

"Did you hear about the hypochondriac's epitaph?" he asked. There was a momentary pause in the chatter while the teenagers considered the question.

Receiving only blank looks, Stuart obliged them with the answer: "I told you I was ill!" I laughed out loud. I was the only one who did! Stuart grinned and explained his joke. It wasn't the best of illustrations—some of these particular English kids weren't sure what an epitaph was!

Epitaphs can be very insightful. I remember walking around an old English graveyard and reading the epitaph on the grave of a Puritan minister: "Here lies the Reverend [So-and-So], who served God for forty years, without enthusiasm." Christians seldom cracked a smile in the Puritan era, as laughter was not considered proper behavior for a sober-minded churchgoer. This was an excellent illustration for a talk I was preparing about the joy of the Lord!

An epitaph on a gravestone is meant to capture the essence of the person who lies beneath it. It purports to tell us about the individual, what he or she was in the judgment of those who knew the person best. It is a reminder of the best elements of character that those who bury the deceased person can find to say about him or her. Perhaps it would be helpful for all of us to spend a little time wondering what our epitaphs might be!

As I studied the life of Moses, God's friend, I had cause to wonder what his epitaph might have been. Moses is revealed as a fearful man, a failing man, and sometimes a furious man. He had a terrible temper that got him into all sorts of trouble throughout his life—trouble with God and trouble with people.

But Moses was also a faithful man, and in the end, God Himself wrote Moses' epitaph. It wasn't written on a tombstone, because we are told that God buried him and didn't put up a marker. "And Moses the servant of the LORD died there in Moab, as the LORD had said. He buried him in Moab, in the valley opposite Beth Peor, but to this day no one knows where his grave is" (Deuteronomy 34:5–6).

Having no tombstone to use as a memorial for future generations, God had others write Moses' epitaph on the leaves of the Bible instead. You can find God's words about Moses in Numbers 12:7–8: "[Moses] is faithful in all my house. With him I speak face to face."

Now, I think you will agree, this is quite an epitaph! I dare to inquire of my own sorry soul: How would my epitaph read if God Himself were to write it? With all his failings, Moses was a faithful man, a friend of God, and as we are told in Numbers

12:3, the humblest person on the face of the earth. Above all, Moses was a man who saw God face-to-face and lived to tell the tale.

Even if we write our epitaphs ahead of time or God writes them for us, someone else will certainly write one for each of us in the end. Somebody will take note of us. It may be a child or grandchild, a friend or enemy, a mother, sister, father, or brother. Who we are and what we did with our lives on this little spinning planet we call Earth will be duly noted and recorded—not only in God's record book but as an epitaph on each of our grave markers. It's a scary thought!

So who was this man Moses, whom the Almighty spoke of with such familiarity and appreciation? Who was this spiritual giant who saw God face-to-face?

Was Moses superhuman? Can we excuse ourselves from seeking to be people of eternal significance and spiritual value because we could never reach Moses' stature? Never scale the heights he reached? Was Moses a near-perfect person? Fortunately for all of us lesser mortals, as we read his story we discover Moses was a man rather like the prophet Elijah, described as "a human being, even as we are" (James 5:17).

Well, now, that's awkward! This means we cannot excuse ourselves from living a life pleasing to and honoring God on the basis that we are wimps when it comes to righteousness, that we are no Moses or Elijah and are therefore free to live spiritually subpar all of our meager lives. If Moses and Elijah are revealed to us as ordinary men who lost their tempers like we do, got discouraged like we do, and blew it like we do, we must accept the fact that God has only imperfect people to use and apparently has decided to use them!

It doesn't take a rocket scientist to see that all God's heroes were very ordinary people. The thing that made the difference was that they had a relationship with an extraordinary God living within them, and this is a privilege accorded to every one of us who recognizes our need to know God in a personal way.

TRANSPORTED INTO TROUBLE

Moses did not have a very promising start to life. He had been transported into Egypt before he was born. The Bible tells us that his forebears came to Egypt during a severe famine. At the time, Egypt had the only grain around, thanks to Joseph's wise management.

Under Joseph, Moses' people had been protected and cared for, but then "Joseph and all his brothers and all that generation died. . . . Then a new king, to whom Joseph meant nothing, came to power in Egypt" (Exodus 1:6, 8). This cruel ruler turned the Hebrew people into slaves.

Moses was not born into a happy world. His parents slaved away for cruel masters who controlled them with whips and worse. Fear was their food. Into this scene of terror and mayhem Moses was born.

Shortly before Moses' birth, Pharaoh, alarmed about the population growth of the Hebrew people, had ordered all newborn boys to be thrown alive into the Nile River. Can you imagine the horror? But God saved the baby Moses in a miraculous way.

The story of how God rescued Moses and used him, along with his brother and sister, is covered in the Bible in Exodus, Leviticus, Numbers, and Deuteronomy. Here you can read how

God saved His people by using Moses, Aaron, and Miriam to lead them out of slavery.

As far as God is concerned, He will get us to the sphere of eternal influence He has in mind for us one way or another. He went to no end of trouble to place three children in Egypt so they would be embedded in enemy territory so He could use them to liberate a people. He transported Moses' family into a whole lot of pain with His plan in mind!

TRANSFORMING THE TRANSFORMERS

God is working on two fronts all the time. As He works to transform society, He works to transform the transformers! God changed Moses, Aaron, and Miriam as they were changing their world.

Here's how it works. God transports us to a situation. There is no such thing as happenstance in the life of a child of God. His intent is to use fallible people to give out His infallible truth to a world living in error. He wants to use weak people who love and obey Him to transform the society to which they have been transported. Then, as we tell others, our own lives are changed in the process.

It is quite exciting to realize we live in the right country at the right time for the right reason, even if the place we were born into, moved to, or traveled to of our own free will is in turmoil. There are three important words on God's mind as He works His will in our world: *location, location, location*! He plants us where He wills in order to fulfill His purposes. So being involved in the global purposes of God gives us a sense of personal purpose as well.

People are looking for a reason for living. Whatever their circumstances, people in every land are searching for the why of their existence. Someone needs to tell them, "This is it!" To know God and be involved in His plan for the human race is what the whole world is really looking for. They just don't know it yet! That's why they are looking in all the wrong places.

People are trying to find permanence as well. They are looking for a safe place to settle down, especially since the 9/11 tragedy and the turmoil brought about with the rise of ISIS. Travel to hot spots is down. Airlines are struggling, and tourism has taken an enormous hit. There are also real and present dangers in our seemingly safe society. A child is stolen from her bedroom. A husband murders his wife. Guns and cars kill thousands. Cancer stalks our homes. Alcohol and drugs make slaves of multitudes.

We look for permanence, but the only permanence is eternal permanence—and only God can give us that! He is the only self-sustaining, permanent being. God can give us eternal life and a permanent place to live in heaven if we ask Him.

TRANSFIGURED

God has a plan for His people that walks right off the edge of this world into the next one. And there is a next one! There is a world beyond this, where flowers never fade, no one ever cries or dies, and no one ever wants to leave. In this bright new world we will be transfigured; "we shall be like him" (1 John 3:2).

One day Jesus took His three closest friends and disciples up a very ordinary mountain to meet some extraordinary people. Suddenly, two men appeared and stood beside Jesus on the mountaintop. The disciples recognized them as Moses and Elijah, who had died hundreds of years before but were obviously very much alive and well when the disciples saw them on the mountain of transfiguration.

Moses and Elijah were talking with Jesus about "his departure, which he was about to bring to fulfillment at Jerusalem" (Luke 9:31). This conversation must have been very confusing to the three disciples.

As the disciples tuned in to the incredible conversation, they began to understand dimly that Moses and Elijah were talking about another exodus: Jesus' exodus out of this present world into the next. They were talking about the cross and resurrection.

Jesus was transfigured in front of their eyes. His face changed, and His clothes shone brightly (Luke 9:28–36). Later, after He rose again from the dead, the disciples understood it all.

Part of God's great and glorious plan is to transport all His disciples into the place of His will to work for Him in this life, to use them to transform the small piece of the planet He holds them accountable for as they find and obey His will. In doing this He will change them from the inside out! The aim of God's grace is to one day welcome us as we accomplish our personal exodus out of this world through death into heaven. Then He will transfigure us by making us like Him. Our "lowly bodies . . . will be like his glorious body" (Philippians 3:21).

So the pattern is for God to get us to the place of His choosing by transporting us by birth, circumstance, or obedience to that chosen location and empowering us to be change agents, and to be changed ourselves, through obedience and the work of His Spirit in our lives. Finally, we will be transfigured and be like Jesus! If we can get hold of this motivating truth, then we stand a good chance of having a halfway decent epitaph written about us.

Are you struggling with the location in which you find yourself? It can't be as bad as Egypt was for Moses! Jesus lived under Caesar, Paul under Claudius and Nero. My husband has often reminded me that it doesn't matter as much who is in the great White House as who is on the "great white throne" (Revelation 20:11)—and we know who that is! There is no circumstance out of God's control. Even a move to another place in the country, around the country, or even out of the country is not without His knowledge!

God transports. Sometimes He transfers us to transform us by our very circumstances. Until our final exodus occurs, we need to be busy being a Moses, Aaron, or Miriam! There is work to do. There are people to tell about the personal transformation and transfiguration possible only through faith in the redeeming grace of God in Christ.

ORDINARY, I UNDERSTAND!

The reason Moses gives me so much hope is that the Bible shows us the failings and phobias of the man. These I can identify with. Ordinary, I understand! Inadequate, I get! I think I can grasp Moses' sense of failure.

All of us feel inadequate in some measure. Whether it is a case of being in over our heads at work, at the bottom of the class in college, a klutz on the sports field, or responsible for an aging and difficult relative in his or her last days, we can all think of a situation in which we come up short.

Perhaps you are trying your best to help an alcoholic parent. You may have been trying to help your parent all your life, but your intentions are misunderstood and unappreciated. Gloria Steinem's situation comes to mind. She said: "I'd already been the very small parent of a very big child—my mother. I felt inadequate then, and I feel inadequate now."[1]

Maybe you are recently divorced and a single parent. You have to confront a teacher at school over a discipline problem with your child and you feel intimidated. Your husband always handled these things! "Here am I, send him," you used to say.

OUR MOSES MOMENTS

There are all sorts of reasons to feel inadequate. One of the main reasons is that you are! Some situations in many of our lives are frankly too much for anyone in the whole world, so it's all right to look at them and say, "Here am I, Lord . . . send somebody else." Of course there might not be anyone else to send, and then you have to decide what to do. This is a Moses moment!

I have a missionary friend who lives in a very dangerous environment overseas. There is a murder each day on her side of town. She is a midwife, so she has to go out in the dark after curfew many times a week. A doctor lives next door. Every time the phone rings, she hesitates to pick it up and finds herself saying to God, "Here am I, Lord . . . send the doctor next door!"

I am a seasoned speaker. I can tell you honestly that after more than fifty years in ministry, when I receive a challenging invitation to speak, I often fight an immediate negative response: "Here am I, Lord . . . send the pastor's wife or that wonderful, young, erudite, and sophisticated speaker I heard last week in church."

I was once invited to talk to a very rich group of women in a country club. I freaked out. I looked at my discount-store dress and shoes, and in my mind's eye I saw the leather- and silk-clad women waiting for me. "Here am I, Lord . . . send my well-dressed friend," I prayed!

There are Moses moments for all of us. The pastor's wife fights comparisons to the "bionic Christian" pastor's wife she followed into the parsonage. The women of the church have invited her to lead the women's ministry, just as the previous pastor's wife did. But she doesn't think she has the same spiritual gifts, and if the truth were known, she doesn't really like women. In fact, she fears she is allergic to people! This is a classic Moses moment.

Do you have Moses moments like this? What do you feel inadequate about?

The less-educated man looks back at his previous boss, who has just retired from the office staff with a ticker-tape parade, and feels he can't possibly measure up. A merger is on the books. He contemplates resigning before he is asked to. This is a Moses moment. Your son's marriage is coming unstuck. You never got along with your daughter-in-law. But now your son has asked you to try to talk to her. This is a Moses moment.

You find out a colleague is having an affair with your best friend. It's none of your business, except your best friend professes to be a Christian and is married! Should you confront her? Should you confront him? This is a Moses moment.

I've had my inadequate moments. Growing up, I felt awkward and ugly in comparison to my beautiful sister, and I knew boys wanted to get to know me only so they could get to know her! When one of her boyfriends showed interest in me, I shunned him, since I didn't want him to be disappointed in me after dating my gorgeous sister. We can feel inadequate a thousand times a day, about a thousand different things.

The release comes when first you realize you are indeed hopelessly inadequate, and then you realize for this you have God! You can't; He can! You are inadequate; He isn't.

How did Moses make it? And did he always make it? The answer to that is: Moses did make it, and he didn't always make it! Remember, he was a human just like us. So what did he do with his Moses moments? How did he get beyond "Here am I, Lord . . . send Aaron"? We'll find out! Maybe if we discover his secret, we will get beyond our own inadequacy too.

A SEARCH FOR IDENTITY

First of all, Moses made it beyond his inadequacy because he had a solid sense of identity. Moses had no problem knowing who he was. And this was surprising, since he was adopted into another race, culture, and family when he was an infant.

As I mentioned earlier in this chapter, Moses was born at a time in history that was possibly one of the most dangerous to be born—if you were a boy, that is. Alarmed at the population growth of the Hebrews, Pharaoh forced them into slavery and then made a decree that all newborn Hebrew boys must be drowned in the Nile River (Exodus 1:22). Moses chose this classic moment to be born.

His parents saw what a beautiful child Moses was and hid

him for three months. Then when it was impossible to hide him any longer, his mother daubed a reed basket with tar, made a lid for it, and told her daughter Miriam to take it to the Nile, put it among the reeds, and wait and see what happened to the baby. I can only imagine Miriam's agony as she obeyed her mother.

The crocodiles must have been very frustrated. A nice meal of baby boy glided tantalizingly past them, but the protective ark encased the child. Moses had never been safer, even though he was yelling fit to raise the mummies—and daddies—in the pyramids! He was on his way to Pharaoh's palace, though he didn't know it. When Pharaoh's daughter came to the water to bathe, her maids saw the basket and took pity on the crying baby. Miriam got ready for action. "This is one of the Hebrew babies," Pharaoh's daughter said (Exodus 2:6).

Miriam ran forward. This was her Moses moment! Her heart must have been beating like mad, but she did not say to God, "Here am I, Lord . . . send my mother, or my father, or my brother Aaron." Instead, she approached the princess and asked if she would like her to find someone to nurse the baby for her. The princess answered, "Yes, go" (v. 8). Miriam raced along the riverbank, her heart still pounding, and brought her mother to Pharaoh's daughter. "Take this baby and nurse him for me, and I will pay you," the princess said to Moses' mother (v. 9).

Can you imagine? Moses was brought up in his own home for a few years until he was weaned. I wonder if the princess ever figured out she had hired the child's own mother. The watching angels must have smiled. When the time came, Moses' mother took him to the palace and handed her baby into the princess's hands. The princess named him Moses (which means "to draw out"), saying, "I drew him out of the water" (v. 10). That day Moses became her child, and he would be brought up an Egyptian.

Though his time with his parents was agonizingly brief, Moses had enough loving prayer and training to know that he was an Israelite. His parents talked about his identity long before little Moses himself could talk! In the years ahead he never forgot who he was and to whom he belonged. He belonged first to God, and then to God's people, the Israelites.

Moses' identity was indelibly written on his soul by a devout family. In the years to come, his sense of identity would be one of Moses' biggest stepping-stones to overcoming his fear and inadequacy.

A LONGING FOR BELONGING

Once we understand we belong to God, a settled assurance begins to permeate our hearts. If we feel inadequate as people, it may be because this issue has never been settled. We may know *about* God, but we don't know if we know *Him*.

Perhaps you have never been introduced. God is so big and we are so small, it's hard to believe such a grand and awesome being would want to know us. But the Scriptures tell us He does want to know us. We are God's workmanship, the work of His fingers (Ephesians 2:10). He created us, and when we ran away from Him, He followed us and offered us a way to reconcile.

A nurse introduced me to God while I was in the hospital. She led me in a simple prayer that went something like this: "Lord Jesus, thank You for coming to earth so You could die for me and bring me back to God. I invite You to invade my life.

Tell my spirit I belong to You. Forgive my sin. I'm sorry. I want to belong to You, amen."

Maybe you would like to borrow my prayer if you have never been introduced to God in a really personal way. You may know about God as I did, but you never have belonged to Him. It's a great thing to find your identity, which comes with your personal introduction to God and to His family. Feel free to stop reading right now and spend time getting this settled.

Many people have a longing for belonging. Once we belong to God, we begin to feel adequate in the face of our problems, however severe they are. You may belong to your family, your friends, your club, or your business. But first you need to belong to God. He made you, and He died for you. You are twice His.

Belonging to Him means you belong to the people of God too. God's "forever family" stretches around the globe. I have met a Christian brother in Vietnam, a sister in Siberia. I have eaten in a relative's home in Jerusalem and another's in Egypt. Not to mention the sisters and brothers I have in Thailand, Europe, and Africa! I belong to God and to His redeemed family all around the world. This gives me a sure and certain sense of my identity. For the Christian, this introduction to God means belonging to the church family.

They say you can't choose your relatives. You can't. You can't choose your church relatives either!

A man I was talking to not long ago told me, "I've left the church."

"You can't," I replied. "Church is not somewhere you go; church is something you are, so you can't leave what you are.

You are a member of the body of Christ! You can't amputate yourself from His body."

I am speaking about both an internal and external belonging. I belonged to a loving family before I came to faith in Christ. I belonged to a group of friends. I belonged to a tennis club and an acting group. I belonged to England. But I didn't belong to God or to His people until I came to faith at the age of eighteen. Once that happened, a sense of belonging possessed me that I had never experienced before. All day long my heart sang a little song I learned at my Bible group:

> Now I belong to Jesus,
> Jesus belongs to me,
> Not for the years of time alone,
> But for eternity.[2]

For the first time in my life I had an inner surety of identity I had never experienced, and that began to create a boldness and courage I had never known. It doesn't mean I stopped having Moses moments. In fact, they were only just beginning! But my sense of belonging and my belief in God helped me maximize those moments, and I found myself stepping out where before I would have shrunk back.

If God were to write your epitaph right now, what do you think it would say? Do you belong to God? Have you become part of His family? Have you ever seen the circumstances of your life—the place you live and the place you work—as part of God's purpose for you? Are you changing your world? Why not? How are you doing with your Moses moments?

It's time to discover, discuss, and then apply the discoveries you have made. If you are using this for your own study time, record your findings in a notebook.

Summary

In a sentence or two, summarize what this chapter is about.

Discovery

Read Exodus 1.

Discussion or Journal

1. All God's heroes were very ordinary people. Do you agree or disagree? What does this say to us?
2. Read Luke 9:28–35. What happened to Moses in the end? What will happen to us?
3. Share a personal Moses moment when you felt very inadequate. How did God help you through that situation?

Decision

1. What truth in this chapter most applies to you?
2. What do you need to do about it?

The Good Doctor
10/9c, ABC

Surgeon Shaun Murphy (Freddie Highmore) is deft with a scalpel, but how's his diapering technique? That's just one skill set Shaun, a medical prodigy on the autism spectrum, will have to master if he and his IT expert live-in girlfriend, Lea (Paige Spara, above, with Highmore), decide to continue the pregnancy revealed in the March 8 episode. "Every year we explore a new challenge, a new opportunity for Shaun," says creator David Shore. "An unexpected pregnancy is both. It's incredibly exciting, but are they ready for this? Is it the right time? We want both Shaun and Lea to explore that."

Much of the episode is devoted to the couple weighing their options, including abortion.

Far from keeping their situation a secret, the compulsively oversharing Shaun and more private Lea invite their colleagues' counsel. "Nobody says, 'Oh, you have to do this' or 'You have to do that,'" Shore promises. "They are true friends in the sense that they go, 'How can I help you better understand what you are feeling and make the best choice for you?'"

Whatever the couple decide, Shore wants to be clear about one thing: "Who Shaun is would make being a parent an additional challenge, but who Shaun is would also make him a *great* parent," he says. "He has an honesty, a candor, a lack of judgment. He wants to do right by people." —*Ileane Rudolph*

THE SPINOFF THAT NEVER HAPPENED!

Charlie's Angels
9/8c, getTV

Retro Pick

In 1980, ABC contemplated a gender-swapped spinoff of its sexy private-eye drama with this episode, "Toni's Boys." But even back then, the wonderfully ludicrous hour played more like a spoof than the setup for a new series. When the Angels (Jaclyn Smith, Cheryl Ladd and Shelley Hack) are targeted by a mobster they testified against (Robert Loggia), Charlie asks his old friend Antonia "Toni" Blake (Barbara Stanwyck) to put her three handsome male detectives on the case. Above, from left, with the Angels, there's Cotton (Stephen Shortridge), the champion rodeo rider and roper who lassos a small plane as it's taking off; former Olympian Bob (Bob Seagren), who polevaults over a high-voltage fence; and "master of disguises and weapons" Matt (Bruce Bauer), who poses as a bearded, vaguely European wine aficionado. Considering they all get

The Curse of Oak Island
9/8c, History

Treasure hunters Rick and Marty Lagina face their yearly dilemma of when to stop digging as the ground begins to freeze in Nova Scotia. But first, the discovery of a new structure near the stone roadway and a possible cannonball cause excitement for the brothers and their crew.

Superman & Lois
9/8c, The CW

Still grieving the loss of Ma Kent, Clark (Tyler Hoechlin) finds a surprising comfort in attending Smallville's Harvest Festival. Sadly, the annual event isn't as celebratory for fire chief Kyle (Erik Valdez), whose less-than-super old habits are getting in the way of his marriage to loan officer Lana (Emmanuelle Chriqui).

HAIR OF THE DOG
Chopped
9/8c, Food Network

Tonight, the competing chefs' "Hangry Baskets" are filled with ingredients people crave when hungover. Hoping for a

Devotion

1. Pray through the discoveries you made while reading this chapter.
2. Pray these same discoveries for others.

A Personal Spiritual Workout

Each day choose a thought or look up a verse or your notes pertaining to the lessons learned and *meditate* (which means to "chew it over") throughout the day. Pray about it each night.

TWO

PALACE TRAINING

No doubt you've heard about the man who was run out of town on a rail and was heard to mutter, "If it wasn't for the honor of the thing, I'd rather not go through with this."

If baby Moses had been aware of his incredible predicament as he lay in his little basket boat among the crocodiles in the Nile, he might well have been tempted to voice similar sentiments! Fortunately, he wasn't aware of his terrible danger. All he could think about was lunch! And like any hungry baby, he cried.

Imagine his baby amazement when his first small, noisy demand wasn't met. All he had known was an immediate response to his every need. After all, his mother, his sister, Miriam, and his brother, Aaron, had danced attention on him from the moment he was born. If Moses had made one sound, all would have been lost. When Pharaoh's soldiers heard the cry of an Israelite baby boy, they would enter the house, take the child, and throw him into the Nile.

Miriam hid in the reeds, watching over her baby brother

and hardly daring to breathe. She was sure a soldier would hear Moses' cries and snatch the little ark her parents had daubed with tar and set among the reeds in the Nile. They were hoping against hope that someone important would find the baby, take pity on him, and rescue him.

So when Moses cried and no one immediately leapt to attention, he was, no doubt, furious! He let out another howl, and perhaps for the first time in his life he was in full voice! And someone did hear him. How good is God!

Of all people, Pharaoh's daughter had come to the river to bathe. Hearing the baby, she sent her maids to retrieve the ark. When she saw the beautiful child in great distress, she was moved. "This is one of the Hebrew babies," she said (Exodus 2:6). Miriam, her heart in her throat, waited to see what would happen to her baby brother. She came out from the reeds and asked the princess if she would like her to find someone to feed the baby. When the princess agreed, you can imagine the speed with which Miriam must have covered the ground to her home!

"Mother, Mother, come quickly! Run!" The frantic urgency in Miriam's face was enough. The two raced along the river-bank, slowing only as they came close to the bend in the river around which they hoped their beloved baby waited in the arms of the princess or one of her maids.

What if Pharaoh's daughter had thought better of her moment of compassion? What if she had thrown baby Moses into the Nile as soon as Miriam had disappeared? After all, she was Pharaoh's daughter! But soon Moses' mother and sister arrived and—miracle of miracles!—Moses was safe and sound.

When the princess told Moses' mother that she would

pay her to care for the baby, Jochabed must have nearly burst with laughter. *Get paid to care for my own baby?* she must have thought. *How good is God!* Now Moses could cry as loud as he liked. The princess would protect him, since this baby one day would be hers. But they would face that reality when the day came, the family decided. With Moses safely back home, the family rejoiced and thanked God, who had worked this miracle for them.

And so it began—the few short years Moses' family was able to love and nurture, pray for, and train their child. They had only a few years to tell young Moses as much as he could possibly understand about God and His people—and much that he wouldn't understand until years later. Moses' parents lived one day at a time, trusting God to take care of their precious child.

God would find His own way to help Moses' family teach him all he needed to know until the day came for his palace training to begin. Parental training would precede palace training. Moses' parents would have to pull out all the stops. They would want Moses to know who he was and what his life was all about. We know they did a great job, for the book of Hebrews records the fruit of their labor of love and faith in detail.

By faith Moses' parents hid him for three months after he was born, because they saw he was no ordinary child, and they were not afraid of the king's edict.

By faith Moses, when he had grown up, refused to be known as the son of Pharaoh's daughter. He chose to be mistreated along with the people of God rather than to enjoy the fleeting pleasures of sin. He regarded disgrace for the sake of

Christ as of greater value than the treasures of Egypt, because
he was looking ahead to his reward. (Hebrews 11:23–26)

Where did Moses learn all that great theology? Not at
the knee of Pharaoh's daughter or the priests of Egypt! Moses
learned from parents full of faith in the living God that he was
loved and planned for by an all-sufficient God.

How would we do things differently with our children if
we knew the urgency that Moses' parents knew? Those of us
charged with training our children for God often believe deep
down we have all the time in the world! Not so. Nobody has all
the time in the world. The experience of baby Moses reminds us
that time is of the essence. Only God knows how brief our time
on earth is, for He has numbered our days.

DON'T UNDERESTIMATE
THE HOLY SPIRIT

Many of us downplay the spiritual importance of the formative
years before our children go to school. We find it hard to believe
children can absorb spiritual truth until they are in grade school.
When I was trained to teach, I was told that children who are
under school age can't understand abstract concepts, such as
the concept of God and His omniscience, omnipotence, and
omnipresence.

I realized later when I was running a Christian preschool
that this assumption was not true. Perhaps it is so in other
dimensions of life, but in the spiritual life the Christian parent has the help of the Holy Spirit to teach, and the child has

the help of the Holy Spirit to learn. Having worked with more than two hundred pupils at a time for ten years and taught the Bible as part of my school curriculum, I am convinced the Holy Spirit explains God and His abstract truth to them. Some of my husband's and my most popular children's books are for preschoolers, and those books are about the incommunicable attributes of God: omnipotence, omniscience, and omnipresence. They get it!

Moses' parents knew exactly how long they had the opportunity to instruct Moses, and they used this precious time to teach their baby boy about spiritual things. Never shortchange what the Holy Spirit does in the lives of small children!

I was in Romania shortly after communism fell. A young woman told me she was brought up in a communist home, but her grandmother was a Christian. Forbidden by her own daughter to talk about God to her grandchildren, the grandmother sought ways around her dilemma.

She used to pull the little girl up on her knee and whisper in her ear, "God loves you!" Then she would put her finger to her lips and say, "Shh!"

After the Berlin Wall came down, a preacher from the West came to her town, stood in the marketplace, and preached the gospel. The young woman's grandmother was dead, but her words lived on. The young woman asked the preacher, "Can you tell me anything about 'the God who loves me'?" She came to faith and went on to lead Christian seminars for women in her country. Never shortchange what the Holy Spirit—and a loving grandmother—can do in the preschool years. As you teach your children, take heart—with the Spirit's help, they get it!

SHAPING MOSES' IDENTITY

So what happened in Moses' case? "When the child grew older, [Moses' mother] took him to Pharaoh's daughter and he became her son" (Exodus 2:10).

I can imagine Moses and his mother were both saying, "If it weren't for the honor of the thing, I'd rather not go through with this!" Perhaps Moses was already saying, "Here am I, Lord . . . send Aaron or Miriam!" But however hard it must have been for young Moses to leave his family, they had all done their work well. His identity had already been shaped.

Moses knew he was a Hebrew. He belonged to the people of God. Moses knew he must love the God who loved him first and supremely! He knew he belonged to the people of God—which meant he was an heir to the promises of God.

God had said that through Abraham all the nations of the earth would be blessed (Genesis 12:3). This meant that Abraham's descendants were wrapped up in the purposes of God to bless the nations. And so it followed that Moses, a descendant of Father Abraham, was too! Moses' identity was with the people of God. And Moses, like his parents, grew up to be a man of faith.

In whatever simple truth it took to relay some of this to young Moses—he apparently got it! Or at least enough of it to know who he was and why he was where he was. His parental education would fit into God's great eternal plan for the nations.

Moses grew up knowing that God made a perfect world, sin spoiled it, and sinners were running it. He knew that God in grace would redeem the fallen world, and those who chose to accept God's forgiveness would receive it and go to heaven. Who knows how well Moses understood all this at such an early age, but like the small Romanian child who had words of life whispered in her ear, Moses kept these things in his heart and the Holy Spirit of truth did the rest.

BELIEVING IN THE INVISIBLE, THE IMPOSSIBLE, AND THE INCREDIBLE

What does it mean to be a man or woman of faith? It means taking a stand with the people of God and for the purposes of God in this world and the next. It means believing in the invisible, the impossible, and the incredible.

Hebrews 11:1 tells us that "faith is confidence in what we hope for and assurance about what we do not see." Faith means being sure and certain about spiritual realities while living in a material world. In other words, it involves believing in the invisible realm of spiritual realities. Moses believed!

"The universe was formed at God's command," and the visible was made from the invisible (v. 3). Things we can see were made from invisible things by an invisible God, whom we can see with the eyes of faith.

This world was made out of invisible things that are now incredibly visible, with God's fingerprints all over them. David said, "When I consider your heavens, the work of your fingers, the moon and the stars, which you have set in place, what is mankind that you are mindful of them, human beings that you care for them?" (Psalm 8:3–4).

The visible world speaks of the invisible God. "Ever since the world was created, people have seen the earth and sky. Through everything God made, they can clearly see his invisible qualities—his eternal power and divine nature. So they have no excuse for not knowing God" (Romans 1:20 NLT). In other words, "He has also set eternity in the human heart" (Ecclesiastes 3:11).

Paul adds:

> God shows his anger from heaven against all sinful, wicked people who suppress the truth by their wickedness. They know the truth about God because he has made it obvious to them. . . . (Romans 1:18–19 NLT)
>
> The basic reality of God is plain enough. Open your eyes and there it is! By taking a long and thoughtful look at what God has created, people have always been able to see what their eyes as such can't see: eternal power, for instance, and the mystery of his divine being. So nobody has a good excuse. (vv. 19–20 THE MESSAGE)

There is another world, other than the one we touch and experience, made out of invisible things and that is still invisible. But it is just as real as the visible one!

After World War II, before any of Europe had time to recover, my father decided we should tour France. This was quite an adventure for my sister and me, and we loved the grand adventure of "car camping"! It was too soon after the peace accords for France's tourist industry to have recovered, so as we motored along we found ourselves sleeping in the car most nights.

One night I woke cramped and restless just before dawn. We were high in the Alps, and I quietly left the family sleeping and went to watch the dawn.

I was fourteen years of age and without Christ. But as I

sat there, I witnessed the invisible God making Himself visible through His "finger work." I ran back to the car, quietly fished around for a pencil and paper, and, sitting on a rock, attempted my first response to His work in my heart, putting it into a poem. It went something like this:

> The dawn breaks softly, filling me with awe.
> It seems the other side of heaven's door.
> That God forgives my sin to me is plain.
> Today in spite of sin
> The sun did rise again!

I was, as Romans says, overwhelmed by the wonders of creation and the Creator, by God's might and my smallness, His holiness and my sin. I had seen enough to be convicted of my need to humble myself and cast myself on His grace. (Had not the sun risen again in spite of my sin?) If I had died at that moment, I would surely have been "without excuse" (Romans 1:20).

All of us have faith training at least from nature, and hopefully also from Christian nurturing.

FAITH TRAINING

Faith means believing in invisible realities and behaving in a way that pleases God. We exist to please Him; He does not exist to please us! It is quite impossible to please God without faith in who He is (Hebrews 11:6).

What is more, God rewards those who come to Him in simple, childlike faith, as Moses did. "He who comes to God must believe that He is and that He is a rewarder of those who seek Him" (Hebrews 11:6 NASB).

If you are a parent or teacher, or if you have children under your influence, are you exposing them to the majesty of God's creation and the grace He offers to us when we give a simple response of faith?

By the time Moses was taken to the palace by his parents, he was sure of God's existence, benevolence, and grace. He was ready for his palace training! Again, Moses' parental training prepared him for the palace, and his palace training prepared him for his work for God. And make no mistake about it: it was not Pharaoh's daughter or even Pharaoh who determined where Moses would be trained; God Himself determined that His deliverer would be trained in Pharaoh's palace.

THE UNIVERSITY OF LIFE

The Bible tells us, "Moses, when he had grown up, refused to be known as the son of Pharaoh's daughter" (v. 24). I wish we knew more about those years. What we do know helps us realize the power of a godly parent's training, faith, and prayer in a child's formative years. Wherever God has allowed you to be brought up and educated, that's His palace of preparation for you. God chooses to school us according to what He has in mind for us in His plan for our lives.

Think about it. Moses needed to be able to read and write. After all, he would be writing a hefty piece of the Bible—in fact, the first five books. And remember, the Bible is the world's best-selling book of all time. Pharaoh may have thought he was preparing Moses for the throne of Egypt, but God had another throne in mind—His own!

One day when Moses' transfiguration was complete, he would cast his crown before his heavenly deliverer and say, "I have finished the work You gave me to do."

We are not delivered from death to work for Pharaoh, or any other earthly power, but to work for God! But, like Moses, our preparation may well be in the palace of a heathen king.

I am thankful for my "palace preparation" in the work that God has given me to do. I see how my education, sports training, and art and drama skills have all been part of the bigger picture, just as Moses' training in languages, government, and leadership were used to keep thousands of people alive while wandering in a desert. Whatever God allows in our lives shapes our identity, affects our choices and value systems, and transforms our behavior.

My palace training gave me a good appreciation of what really matters in life and a persevering faith that sees the invisible reality and looks forward to life eternal and the rewards of grace. The rewards of grace, not greed, are what really count.

Our palace training shapes us. Whatever happens to us is part and parcel of making us who we are. Everything that goes into making us the people we are—our childhood, adolescence, education, nationalities, and spiritual environments—is part of our palace training. God sends us to the university of life and uses everything to make us into people He can use.

As we prepared to immigrate to America in 1970, I remember warning our children that Americans might think their English accents were strange and make fun of them. But when we arrived, I discovered that, on the contrary, their English accents made them celebrities! People would hide behind a pillar in church just so they could hear them talk. Our accents were part of our palace training, and they gave us an instant entry into conversation and relationships. I found that my training in word skills in Britain now began to be used in speaking and writing in America. But other things began to help us all to adjust as well.

It came as a surprise to me that the children's culture had been completely different in Britain. Weren't Americans and the British supposed to be the same? Yet they were not the same at all! As Winston Churchill was purported to say, "The British and the Americans are one people separated by a common language."

Not only was the language different in America, but Americans had a different way of living life. Our children had been taught to make their own choices much earlier than their counterparts had. There were no counselors in British schools, for example. The children were responsible for their choices and knew it. They decided what to do in moral dilemmas, and they were conscious of the fact they lived with the consequences of their own choices. They didn't blame anyone else.

BEHAVIOR FLOWS OUT OF BELIEF

Moses was on his own in Pharaoh's palace, apart from his Egyptian trainers. Yet early training had given him the option of making right choices by himself at an early age. This faith training from his youngest years affected how Moses behaved.

When it was time to make life-changing choices, Moses chose rightly. For example, he renounced sonship and kingship on earth for his reward in heaven. Moses was so sure of unseen realities, he renounced the pleasures of sin he could see with his physical eyes for pleasures in the spiritual realm he couldn't see with his physical eyes—the pleasures of salvation. His faith shone bright and clear, as evidenced by his moral choices and his lifestyle (Hebrews 11:24–26).

What Moses believed affected how he behaved—as it should for all of us! Moses was a man of integrity. He discovered that life is a series of choices and that our behavior flows out of our belief. What we believe determines what we choose to do in life, and some of these hard choices may cause us grief.

There are opposing forces of good and evil in our world: God and Satan. Sometimes Satan appears as an angel of light. He presents sin as a pleasure, and, make no bones about it, sin often brings temporary pleasure. After all, the Devil did not offer Eve a rotten apple. He didn't tempt David with an ugly woman or Bathsheba with an ugly man, either.

A DRINK OF SALT WATER

The Devil is careful not to tell us that he can't sustain sin's temporary pleasure. Even the apple will be eaten after a while. The Devil's fun doesn't last; it is addictive and leaves you always wanting more. Living in sin is like being thirsty and being given a drink of salt water. It temporarily satisfies but leads to raging thirst and the torture of only more salt water!

So Moses chose pain over pleasure. The pain of identifying with God's people would be for only a short time; the true pleasures of belonging to God would last forever. "In your presence there is fullness of joy; at your right hand are pleasures forever-more" (Psalm 16:11 ESV).

A SYSTEM OF VALUES

Making good judgments is important in life. And your judg-ments, whether good or bad, are based on your system of values, which comes from family, society, or God.

Tradition says that when little Moses had spent a short time in the palace, he threw down his crown at the feet of Pharaoh. This may or may not be true. Perhaps little Moses enjoyed the pleasures of the royal home as any other prince would, but when he reached the age of forty, he had figured it out. "By faith, Moses, when grown, refused the privileges of the Egyptian royal house. He chose a hard life with God's people rather than an opportunistic soft life of sin with the oppressors" (Hebrews 11:24–25 THE MESSAGE).

The pleasures and treasures of Egypt represent all the world can offer us without God at the center. The apostle John tells us, "Do not love the world or anything in the world. If anyone loves the world, love for the Father is not in them. For everything in the world—the lust of the flesh, the lust of the eyes, and the pride of life—comes not from the Father but from the world. The world and its desires pass away, but whoever does the will of God lives forever" (1 John 2:15–17).

My husband says that the cravings, the coveting, and the crowing outlined in this passage equate to our passions, posses-sions, and position. Passion can mean sex without boundaries or accountability. It can mean desire that is out of control in many dimensions of our lives. Loving the world has to do not only with our possessions, but with our position and ambitions. When our own fame, glory, and honor mean more to us than God's, we are in danger of worldliness.

The palace must have been a huge temptation for Moses. We might not live in a palace, but I think the love of the world can be a huge temptation for us too!

In his book *Celebration of Discipline*, Richard Foster says,

> The modern hero is the poor boy who purposely becomes rich rather than the rich boy who voluntarily becomes poor. . . . Covetousness we call ambition. Hoarding we call prudence. Greed we call industry. . . . Owning things is an obsession in our culture.[1]

We are all fascinated with the lifestyles of the rich and famous. Wealth, we are told, is the benchmark of achievement. It does not seem to be a question of how much character you have but how much cash!

The Devil offered Jesus the world and all its treasures, but Jesus refused to give in to this temptation. He realized the catch: you have to worship the Devil to get these treasures! The Devil may be the prince of this world, but Jesus said, "My kingdom is not of this world" (John 18:36). Jesus chose the higher ground. So did Moses. He chose to worship and serve God and not the Devil, to work for God's eternal reward and not an earthly crown. It was all part of Moses' identity as a child of God.

At any time of the day or night, we are faced with a choice: to identify with this world or to remember whom we serve. You may have to make this choice at a party when things get out of hand, at a business meeting where something less than truthful is being spoken, or at a schoolyard where you find yourself with your back against a wall. Hopefully your choices will reflect whose you are and whom you serve—as Moses' choices did.

Moses looked forward to the coming Messiah, as had Abraham. And like Abraham, Moses tried to live his life in the present in the light of the future. As Jesus once told a group of religious leaders, "Your father Abraham rejoiced at the thought of seeing my day; he saw it and was glad" (John 8:56).

A healthy sense of identity comes from belonging to God through Christ and choosing to work for God's purpose and plan, not yours. If you choose to obey God, you will likely encounter opposition and hardship, and you will certainly have to practice self-denial. It doesn't mean you will always rise to the occasion either! In fact, Moses' first grand attempt to make an impact for God led to disaster, as we will see in the next chapter.

It's time to discover, discuss, and then apply the discoveries you have made. If you are using this for your own study time, record your findings in a notebook.

Summary

In a sentence or two, summarize what this chapter is about.

Discovery

Read Exodus 2.

Discussion or Journal

1. If you knew you had only four years with a small child, what five things would you make sure that child knew about the Lord and him- or herself? Make a list.
2. Share something of your own "palace training" that has stood you in good stead as a Christian.
3. Discuss the following statement: Behavior flows out of belief.

Decision

1. What truth in this chapter most applies to you? What do you need to do about it?
2. Do you believe in the invisible world of spiritual realities? What is your current level of faith and trust in God?

Devotion

1. Pray through the discoveries you made while reading this chapter.
2. Pray for these same discoveries for your family.

A Personal Spiritual Workout

Each day choose a thought or look up a verse in Hebrews 11 and *meditate* (which means to "chew it over") throughout the day. Pray about it each night.

THREE

DELIVERED TO
BE A DELIVERER

If you have been discouraged by your first attempt to deliver someone, take heart! Though Moses delivered thousands of his people from oppression in Egypt, his first attempt to deliver someone resulted in a terrible tragedy.

One day when Moses was grown, he saw one of his people being beaten by a slave master. Moses was outraged by the beating and killed the Egyptian, burying him in the sand. The next day, when Moses saw two Israelites scrapping and tried to stop them, one of them said, "Who made you ruler and judge over us? Are you thinking of killing me as you killed the Egyptian?" Then Moses realized that his murder of the Egyptian had become known and feared for his life (Exodus 2:11–14).

Out of the palace, Moses went to find someone to save, and he didn't have to look very far! Now he would begin the task God had entrusted to him. In his well-meaning but misguided attempt,

Moses saved his brother Jew but lost his brother Egyptian. What a start to Moses' delivering ministry! His first attempt to deliver someone ended in murder. But God's preparation of His deliverer was not complete. Moses may have been prepared in the palace, but a lot more was needed.

DESERT TRAINING

So, Moses identified with the people of God and the plan of God, but his first attempt to deliver one of his people ended in disaster! When Pharaoh heard about the murder, he tried to kill Moses, but Moses fled to Midian, which was in the desert.

Events such as these, which are recorded in the Old Testament, are often used in the New Testament to make a spiritual point. One valid analogy paints Egypt as a place where people are slaves and need to be set free, just as the human race is enslaved to sin and needs to be released from spiritual bondage.

Moses was delivered from Egypt in order to be a deliverer for others. He would be used by God to lead the people out of slavery, through the Red Sea, and into Canaan, a land flowing with milk and honey. But God's leaders need to be trained, and often that training takes place in the school of life!

The analogy of being saved out of Egypt is an analogy of being delivered into freedom, rest, security, and prosperity in every dimension. So it's valid to use this picture in Scripture and compare it to our own spiritual journey, especially since the Bible itself tells us what this analogy means.

Let us pause for a moment and apply this. Everybody starts in a place similar to Egypt. We are born into a world belonging to a prince who does not acknowledge Christ and is vehemently antagonistic to Him. Let us think of Pharaoh as representing Satan, who rules the nations of the world in which we live. Jesus acknowledged Satan's kingdom and called him "the prince of this world" (John 14:30). Behind the Egyptian Pharaoh in the book of Exodus stands this evil prince.

At the age of eighteen, living in England, I considered myself a Christian simply because I was born in a Christian country. It was not until I was old enough to feel the restraining chains of my slavery that I became aware that I had been born in "Egypt" and didn't know it, and "Pharaoh" controlled my world and my life.

MASTERED BY OUR TASKS

Pharaoh controlled the people in Egypt by putting taskmasters over them. Scripture tells us that the Egyptians "put slave masters over them to oppress them with forced labor, and they built . . . store cities for Pharaoh" (Exodus 1:11).

Satan has his taskmasters too. He uses tasks that master us until we find ourselves burdened with things that we come to believe *have* to be done or our world will fall apart. As someone has said, "We have become human doings, not human beings."

Think for a moment about the things you are busy doing. Have your tasks so mastered you that you have become burdened and distracted by them? The problem might be that you have been kept so busy you haven't ever thought about it. Affliction may have come to your family simply because you have had to obey your taskmaster. Surely you are producing; you are even building cities! You are achieving visible results, but they're all for Pharaoh. The tasks that are busying you are not building a better relationship with your spouse and children or making you more effective in your friends' lives or helping you to know God!

It's just as if all that work is producing a treasure city for other people to enjoy. You sweat it out, and they take all the credit and have the enjoyment of your labor. You have nothing to show at the end. Oh, you may have a brick or two that Pharaoh allowed you to keep for wages, but in the end you will leave it all behind, for it is his. He is the prince of this world, and everything here belongs to him.

When a wealthy acquaintance died, I asked my husband about the deceased man's will.

"How much did he leave?" I asked.

"Everything!" my husband replied.

True, and as God asked in the parable of the rich fool, "Fool! Tonight you die. Then who will get it all?" (Luke 12:20 TLB). Are we building treasure cities for Pharaoh that will have to be left behind, or are we building something lasting in heaven?

A story is told of a wealthy man who labored with many tasks here on earth and produced beautiful palaces in which he lived sumptuously, though selfishly, all his life. This man accepted Christ on his deathbed. He had a gardener whose life did not "consist in an abundance of possessions" (v. 15). The gardener had come to know God, he had been personally set free, and his treasure was in heaven.

Both died and went into eternity. The gardener was given a beautiful mansion in heaven. It had a marvelous view of the Sea of Glass, in full view of the Throne. The rich man was offered a hut—clean and white, but just a hut! Seeing his face fall, the apostle Peter explained, "I'm sorry, sir, but we did the best we could with the materials you sent up!"

What are you and I busy building? Who are our taskmasters? What have we achieved of eternal worth? Let me tell you something: You will never build anything in heaven while you are in bondage in Egypt. You will come to the place where your tasks master you, and the whole thing becomes a bitter burden. Your taskmasters will drive you faster and faster. If only they would give you time to think, you would realize you were not created to be a slave of Pharaoh, but a servant of God.

A CHANGE OF MASTERS
IS IMPERATIVE

There came a time in my own experience when I recognized that I was mastered. I had rationalized my sin and called it "growing up," simply because I would not admit to belonging to Pharaoh! My taskmasters kept me so busy I could take no time to think. In the end, the burden was so great that I realized I had done nothing of eternal worth up to that point in my life.

Created to serve Jehovah, I served another master, even though I knew that God said, "You shall have no other gods before me" (Deuteronomy 5:7). No one was better off because I had been around; no one was helped or blessed heaven for knowing me. True, I was friendly with some other slaves, but the only sharing we ever did was to rattle our chains in fellowship or help each other build something else for Pharaoh. I discovered I needed delivering!

As I mentioned in chapter 1, one day I said a simple prayer and God began to get things in order in my life. I used different language, but in essence I prayed something like this:

Oh God, You tell me I am born in Egypt—or born in sin. Satan has me where he wants me and I belong to him. I realize I'm captive to taskmasters who have kept me so busy I haven't even had time to think about the things that really matter—like You!

But I've come to the point where I'm so pressured by it all, I've stopped long enough to feel the sting of the whip and acknowledge my need of deliverance. I need help! As You provided a deliverer for the children of Israel, I read in the Bible that You have provided one for me. His name is Jesus, and I call on Him right now. Hear me, Lord. Save me from Pharaoh and from living a wasted life. Enter my heart by Your Holy Spirit, and set me free to serve another Master, whose service is perfect freedom, amen.

If we realize our position and cry to God by reason of our troubles, as the children of Jacob did, God will hear us and remember the promises He made to our forefathers. He will look, and He will see. He knows our plight and has provided a way of escape. At the age of eighteen, I looked for and found the provided Deliverer and became sure of my identity for the first time. I didn't belong to my selfish self; I belonged to God.

DESERT EXPERIENCE BEFORE DELIVERING EXPERIENCE

I instinctively knew I was saved to serve and blessed to be a blessing. I had no idea how to go about it, just as Moses had no idea how to go about it. I just went out into my college world and began to try to deliver people! Like Moses, I immediately discovered I needed to make some lifestyle changes before anyone would listen to me. As Moses had to deal with his temper, I had to deal with my arrogance and pride. I knew how to do this work, I decided. But the people I was trying to "save" had the same response as the Israelite arguing with his fellow Israelite, who looked at Moses and asked, "Who made you ruler and judge over us?" (Exodus 2:14).

I didn't murder anyone, but I killed a few people's interest in a hurry! I was using my "palace training" of talents and communication skills, but I badly needed some desert training.

Moses, too, needed a desert experience before anyone else could have a delivering experience. That's how it works.

A MODEL OF GROWTH AND LEARNING

Moses' problem was his temper. He simply could not control it. You will never liberate anyone else if you have not experienced some measure of liberation yourself. Moses had to deal with his lack of self-control before he could ever be entrusted with the pastoral care of God's people. The Lord knew how many times in the future Moses would be stretched to the limit of his patience with the grumbling, mumbling children of Israel, and since it would take them forty years to enter the promised land, God had to liberate Moses from that problem!

I am not saying that we have to achieve perfection before we can begin our work for God, but we have to see little steps to victory along the way. Moses was never completely liberated from his terrible temper, but he learned enough self-control to achieve God's goal for him. After all, we are not expected to be models of perfection, but models of growth and learning.

Remember when Moses came down from the mountain of God with the Ten Commandments in his hands and found his people prostrating themselves in front of the golden calf (Exodus 32:19)? Do you remember what he did? That's right—he lost his temper and broke the Ten Commandments. (You always do, you know, when you lose your temper!) But progress had definitely been made. Moses did not break the stone tablets over the people's heads; he broke them on the ground. Then he went back to God to start all over again. He had learned that in the desert.

It took God forty years to prepare His deliverer to be a deliverer, so take heart. Don't go rushing out to save someone as soon as you become a believer. Spend some time waiting for God to show you His time and His way, and allow Him to mature you a little bit.

Before you start sharing your testimony, be prepared to let God begin to do some changing work in your heart so you are not speaking with great authority from the depths of your ignorance. Otherwise, you will just end up hurting someone. This is what the desert is for. John the Baptist was in the desert until the time for his public ministry (Luke 1:80). God told him when to start, and it was just the right moment.

You see, there's no avoiding the fact that it takes time to prepare a deliverer. It takes other things, too, such as crocodiles, bulrushes, palaces, and choosing to say no to the pleasures of sin. Preparing a deliverer takes failure, fear, flight, and forgiveness; and it will probably take a burning bush experience in the desert of your disappointments as well.

MEMORIES, MONOTONY, AND MARRIAGE

When Moses fled to the desert, he met a family who cared for him. The priest of Midian, a man named Reuel, gave Moses his daughter Zipporah in marriage, and Moses settled down to shepherding the flocks of his father-in-law (Exodus 2:16–21). What a seemingly sad end to a promising career! But it was all part of God's training of a great deliverer for the people of Israel. God uses such ordinary things to prepare us for effective service. For example, God uses our memories. God knew that Moses would someday have to lead thousands of people who had endured the horrendous experience of slavery. How could God's people find healing and help for all their memories of slavery in Egypt? Well, Moses had a few gruesome memories of his own, and God wanted him to deal with them so he could help others deal with them too.

Moses had to forgive himself for being the murderer God had already forgiven him for being. He had to learn, as we have to learn, that God has forgiven and forgotten our sins, and what God has forgotten we have no right to remember. God has said, "I will forgive their wickedness and will remember their sins no more" (Hebrews 8:12). As we learn how to allow God to deal with our past, we can help others deal with theirs.

YOU CAN'T BE SPIRITUALLY PRODUCTIVE IF YOU ARE GUILT RIDDEN

Guilt is a robber. Satan uses guilt to rob you of God and to rob God of you. But God wants us to allow guilt to drive us to Him, not away from Him. Guilt can be all-absorbing. You become so self-absorbed and controlled by your bad memories, other people don't even figure in your thoughts. What freedom it is to realize that there is no sin too big for God to forgive. Finding freedom and forgiveness in Christ has given me a relevant message for this generation of guilt-ridden people.

Moses not only had to learn to deal with his guilt, but he also had to learn to allow monotony to shape his character. I don't suppose there are many more monotonous tasks than forty years of keeping sheep in a desert. Meditation is one antidote for monotony, and I'm sure Moses learned to stay his mind on a God who holds the mysteries of heaven ready to reveal to anyone who has the time and inclination to unravel them. This exercise would sharpen Moses' wits and inspire his thoughts, and so deal with the monotony of his occupation.

Moses surely learned what to do with solitude while in the desert of Midian. In our noisy world, we hurried people are threatened by the concept of being alone and quiet. Tuning into the quiet places of the soul must have been strange to Moses at first, considering the teeming streets of Egypt and the palace full of people where he had grown up.

Sometimes God has to physically place us in such an environment of solitude so we can discover Him. It may be a stay in an isolated hospital room, a vacation in the remote woods, or a spell in another country where you can't speak the language and experience a desert of communication that makes you feel very alone. If we can accept these situations as a gift and maximize the use of silence to know God and His purposes better, we will be well on our way to being a help to others.

THE DAILY DAY

Even in his monotonous environment, Moses had opportunities to speak of the God to whom he belonged. There is no doubt his extended desert family in Midian heard all he could tell them about the Lord God of his father Abraham. The shepherds Moses met surely learned about the grace and goodness of God from the Egyptian who explained he was an Israelite living as a Midianite!

Moses also married during his stay in the desert. I'm sure God knew he was going to need a little understanding of the ways and wiles of the fairer sex. And he would need to experience the problems of family life if he was ever to be counselor and friend to a city of families without a city. It's hard enough to help families who have a home and a measure of security; but what do you do when you wander around for forty years with thousands of families at your back? Moses surely needed some personal experience in the matter of marriage. And so in these three areas—memories, monotony, and marriage—God prepared His man.

It is in this university of the mundane that we become the people God can use. Yes, theological training is icing on the cake, but most of us will have to settle for a cake with little or no icing at all! Start to think about the lessons of usefulness learned in the backside of whatever wilderness you are experiencing. You'll see, someone is waiting for you to bless him or her with your experience of God in the wilderness!

That's good news for you and me, isn't it? If I can take my palace education and marry it to some desert experience, I have begun to grow into a person God can use. If I can learn to appreciate forgiveness, beat monotony with meditation, and use the lessons of my relationships at home to give me a greater sympathy and understanding of others, then I'm well on the way to being the deliverer I was delivered to be. You see, not every born-again believer is a preacher or a teacher, but every true Christian is committed to Christ and needs to be committed to others who are still in Egypt and need to be saved to serve.

WHEN GOD COMES CALLING

God listens to the cry of His people. He listens to the cry of the unbeliever who needs to be set free from sin and Satan, and He listens to the cry of the believer who knows better but is still living in slavery when he could be free! Salvation is a continuous experience. It starts with an exodus from Egypt but continues through the desert of the world until we see God in heaven face-to-face.

Both Christians and non-Christians need the saving life of God to liberate them and keep them free. When God saw the incredible cruelty His people were experiencing, He came calling. He knew exactly where to look for the man He would use. In fact, God had been preparing Moses for eighty years to be the deliverer of Israel. When the time was right for Moses to know God's plan for him, God chose a place and a time and came to visit.

One pivotal day, Moses, who probably believed he would retire in a tent in the middle of nowhere, set off to work only to get the shock of his life. He had no way of knowing what was happening back in Egypt! But God knew, and having listened to people desperately praying for help miles away, God decided it was time to answer those urgent prayers for salvation. The Lord would soon tell Moses, "I have indeed seen the misery of my people in Egypt. I have heard them crying out because of their slave drivers, and I am concerned about their suffering" (Exodus 3:7). I love the way God not only sees people's needs, but He knows the right person to address that need. God isn't hampered by distance or circumstance, and He will work to bring the two together.

I think about my own experience. I was a student at college and fell ill one night. I was rushed to the hospital and placed in a large ward next to the first Christian I was aware of meeting in so-called Christian England! I was the seeking soul. She was the willing worker. She had been prepared in both the palace and the desert to help me.

How did God get us together? He used an event He had allowed to happen in her life—an accident at work—to put her in the bed next to me. The placing and timing were perfect. I was frightened and open to being helped. She had the help ready and was willing for God to use her. She led me to Christ!

She didn't say, "God has allowed this terrible thing to happen to me. Poor little me!" She accepted the fact that accidents happen in life, and she looked for anyone around her to whom she could be a burning bush. She found me! There I was, right in the middle of my desert wanderings, lost and without hope. Then God came calling. I noticed something unusual about this girl, and as Moses "turned aside" to see why the scrub bush was burning (v. 4 KJV), I did the same. I discovered—miracle of miracles!—that God was in the midst of the bush. Before I left the hospital, I was a burning bush too!

A VEHICLE TO DEMONSTRATE GOD'S LIFE

The first thing we need to learn about this work of helping others out of Egypt and into Canaan is that God is looking for very scrubby scrub bushes. The scrubbier the better, because then the fire burns fiercer and brighter! He looks for availability too. Let us summarize Exodus 3:1–5. This very scrubby little scrub bush was simply sitting right under Moses' nose, minding its own business, when God decided to use it for a very special purpose.

Maybe you can identify. Perhaps you feel like a little scrub bush in a remote area of the desert. You are no different from a thousand other little scrub bushes. You think you are not important at all—except, of course, to the other scrub bush that sits close to you in your desert world. But listen, little scrub bush, God can use you! You are growing in just the right place.

What for? Sometimes it is to shine brightly for an unbeliever, and sometimes it is to light up the darkness of a believer's soul. In this instance, God's chosen deliverer was wandering around with a lot of scraggy sheep for company in the desert. He was defeated, discouraged, disappointed, and possibly depressed.

Moses needed to be diverted so the people could be converted. But how?

Well, God needed a vehicle to demonstrate His life. A little scrub bush was perfect! This way God could show us that He can use anything or anyone for His purposes. And that's just what God did.

God had to somehow catch His man's eye. And as the noted Bible speaker Major Ian Thomas stated, "Any old bush will do!" In fact, God likes to use things and people that really are very ordinary to let others see the extraordinary contrast of God's presence within them. This way God gets all the glory, which is how it must be.

Ability is nice, such as the ability to win an argument or the ability to witness to a stranger, but availability is all-important! We need to go out into our day telling God that we are available to burn brightly wherever and whenever He needs us.

THE FIRE IS GOD'S

Let me adapt Major Ian Thomas's statement by saying, "Any old bush can burn." The little scrub bush that diverted the deliverer's attention was demonstrating a truth that Moses needed to be reminded of. The truth was that the fire was God's! The writer of Hebrews stated, "Our 'God is a consuming fire'" (12:29). He also stated that God "makes . . . his servants flames of fire" (1:7).

The dejected Christian who has run away from his work and feels worthless needs to be confronted by someone who hasn't run away and is demonstrating a life in which the Holy Spirit burns with a consistency that demands investigation. How can a bush burn? Only by the hand of God. If God can use a little scrub bush, then He can use a forgiven murderer!

When Moses turned aside to see the little scrub bush, he saw it was burning but not burning up. He not only found out that "any old bush will do" and "any old bush can burn," but he also discovered that "any old bush can speak"! The Lord spoke from the heart of the bush.

One day, not many months later, the quiet of the vast desert was shattered as thousands of God's people tramped past a very insignificant thorn bush on their way to Canaan. If the little scrub bush could have waved and rejoiced, it would surely have done so. In a very real way, God had used that insignificant bush to divert His deliverer and send him on his way to do His will.

Even if I can never be a Moses, I can surely be a scrub bush and allow God to speak to others from my heart. What words does God speak from your heart? Words of hope and renewal? Words of life and joy? Our job is to not quench the Spirit's fire and to be aware that a Moses may enter our lives today! This may have been the only opportunity the scrub bush had to be used in such an incredible way. It's not a matter of how many times God uses us, but that God does use us when and how He chooses. Giving God permission to do so is the beginning point of ministry.

My mother-in-law, who is now a resident of heaven, was used only once, as far as she knew, to lead someone to Christ. She had no way of knowing she was delivering a deliverer! That seven-year-old boy was just an ordinary little boy, and no one could know that forty years later Stuart Briscoe would be used throughout the world to lead many, many people out of Egypt into Canaan. As I have had the privilege and joy of watching that particular bush burn for more than sixty years, I know one person is not more important than the other. Each to his task, that's all.

Stuart and his mother did not compete for a reward based on the numerical results of their ministries. One bush may have a greater capacity to reveal Christ to the world than another, but we are all nothing without Christ, and again, "any old bush can burn"! The incredible thing to me is that God uses the "foolish things of the world to shame the wise; . . . the weak things of the world to shame the strong. God chose the lowly things of this world and the despised things—and the things that are not—to nullify the things that are" (1 Corinthians 1:27–28). That seems incredible until I read verse 29 and find the reason: "that no one may boast before him."

So whether you are a Moses or a scrub bush, will you burn for God? A deliverer must be diverted so the people may be converted! Your time may have arrived. Perhaps your preparation is complete and it's time to take off your shoes, as Moses did before the burning bush. You need to be very careful how and where you walk from now on, for the place where you stand, when you finally face up to your call and your responsibilities, is holy ground.

Maybe some who read these words would like to burn but are afraid. It sounds rather uncomfortable—all that fire and smoke and flames! Perhaps there are some crooked parts of your scrub bush you like too well, and you don't want them to be destroyed. *If I let God set me alight with His presence, what will be left?* you wonder. Notice what the Bible says about the scrub bush: "though the bush was on fire it did not burn up" (Exodus 3:2). How invigorating is the fire of God that He imparts to those who choose to choose what He has chosen for their lives! So turn aside to see, won't you?

TURNING ASIDE TO SEE

What would have happened to Moses or the Israelites if Moses had not "turned aside to see" (v. 4 KJV)? Deliverance would have come for the Jews from another direction. Maybe Aaron would have been God's choice. Moses would have missed out, that is for sure! But a spiritual curiosity to discover God's plan for our lives is essential if we are to hear and obey God's calling for us.

How do we go to church: in a listening mode or a critical one? Do we talk to other church bushes and pass the time of day, or do we speak to one another in love, talking often of the things of the Lord and spurring each other on to godliness and good works? Do we hang around any burning bush we can see, excited to hear from the pulpit of their hearts?

Whatever mess you have made in life, let the story of Moses encourage you to be aware of God in the ordinary things of life and learn to watch for Him, listen for Him, and learn from Him. Failure is never final for the Christian, and there is a world to be won for the Lord. There are also plenty of people like Moses who need to be encouraged back into usefulness. All you have to do is turn aside daily to see the things of God for yourself, and then burn brightly on. Be assured, if the fire is God's, and not your own flames of self-energy, you will burn on and not burn out. And who knows—a Moses might be saved for kingdom work!

Some reading this chapter may feel they have been sidelined

by a mistake they made in the past and are marking time until God takes them home. God lives in the desert as well as the town. He is ever concerned about our well-being. Even if it has been forty years, be encouraged to believe there is life after failure. Turn aside to see. Turn aside to listen. Your life will never be the same!

It's time to discover, discuss, and then apply the discoveries you have made. If you are using this for your own study time, record your findings in a notebook.

Summary

In a sentence or two, summarize what this chapter is about.

Discovery

Read Exodus 3.

Discussion or Journal

If we will not choose to go with God to a desert place apart, He will lead us or drive us there.

1. Discuss the reasons people will not spend the time with God that it takes to become spiritually mature.
2. Share some personal hard lessons learned about service without preparation.
3. Look up the following verses concerning the

desert habits of our Lord Jesus. Read them out loud in the group: Matthew 26:36; Matthew 4:1; Matthew 14:23; Luke 6:12.

God shapes us for His service not only in the palace but also in the desert, with some very ordinary tools. Do you remember just three of these tools I suggested to you? God not only used these shaping circumstances in Moses' life, but I suspect He uses them in ours also. They were memories, monotony, and marriage.

1. Share with the group how any of these has *prevented you* from being a deliverer and why.
2. Share how experiences within these areas have contributed to making you a *better deliverer*.
3. Discuss the following statement: "I have to have complete victory over bad habits in my life before I can witness to the people in Egypt." (Remember Moses.)

Decision

1. Turn to 1 Corinthians 1:26–31. Make a list of the qualifications of the man or woman that God has called.
2. Why does God choose such scrub bushes (v. 29)?
3. What in this chapter most applies to you?
4. What do you need to do about it?

Devotion

Try to get alone and think about the life you have lived so far. Which part of this chapter most accurately applies to you? Ask God to develop a healthy spiritual curiosity in you to find out God's purpose for your life. Maybe you could make a list of the life lessons you have learned about monotony, meditation, and marriage that could be used to help others.

1. Ask yourself, is there real fire in my life, or am I just burning up my own energy? Am I burned out? If so, why?
2. What are people hearing from the pulpit of your heart?
3. Pray about all you have been talking about in your group or recording in your journal. Keep your prayers short, to the point, and honest.
4. Pray for any "Moses" you know.

A Personal Spiritual Workout

Each day choose a thought or look up a verse or your notes pertaining to the lessons learned, and *meditate* (which means to "chew it over") throughout the day. Pray about it each night.

FOUR

BETWEEN THE DEVIL
AND THE DEEP RED SEA

L et My people go," demanded God through the lips of
Moses and Aaron.

"Why should I?" responded Pharaoh, behind whom stood
the enemy of men's souls.

As soon as the demands were made, the situation worsened
for the Israelites. Pharaoh tightened his grip on them and told
the taskmasters to make the Israelite slaves' lives even more
miserable than before. He said, "Make the work harder for the
people so that they keep working and pay no attention to lies"
(Exodus 5:9).

When we are trying to deliver people "out of Egypt," it may
seem at first as if things get worse. This can almost be a good sign
for us when we are praying for loved ones, for as we come in prayer in
the name of Jehovah God, seeking to demand that Pharaoh release
the slaves he controls, we can expect him to do just what Pharaoh

did and tighten his grip. Pharaoh and his army usually show up if we get serious about winning people to God's cause. The Bible tells us not to be ignorant of the Devil's devices (2 Corinthians 2:11), so we need to know how to watch out for them.

I remember the Reverend Dick Rees, a pastor in Britain, speaking about how he witnessed to his brother, Tom. Tom became antagonistic toward the gospel and toward his brother, the gospel's messenger. In fact, the more people prayed for him, the worse Tom's attitude became. He not only wouldn't listen to Dick, but he became even more bitter, just like the Israelites, who "did not listen" to Moses "because of their discouragement and harsh labor" (Exodus 6:9).

This apparent hardening of attitude tells us something. Satan is worried. So pray on, and believe that soon they will be free. We must believe God for their freedom. We must believe for those who cannot believe for themselves.

Pharaoh wouldn't listen to God's representative, and neither would the children of Israel. So God decided to add another voice: the voice of the plagues. God is in charge of the world that He created. He controls its laws, and He can interrupt and reverse them at will. He controls the creatures He made. Sometimes God manifests His power through nature in order to bring men and women to realize His power and authority.

Exodus 7–8 tells us that water became blood, and the Nile teemed with frogs that came into the Egyptians' houses, into Pharaoh's palace, and even into people's beds! The magicians of Egypt mimicked some of these miracles, but there came a point where they could no longer work their magical arts. Yet Pharaoh was not persuaded in his heart that this was "the finger of God," and he remained adamantly opposed to any Israelite demands.

SERVING GOD IN EGYPT

Moses and Aaron went to Pharaoh again and asked him to let the people travel away from Egypt into the desert to worship God.

"Let my people go, so that they may worship me," God demanded through His mouthpiece (Exodus 8:1). As Jesus said, "No one can serve two masters" (Matthew 6:24). We have been told that we should serve God *only* (Matthew 4:10). The problem with many people today is that they think they can serve God in Egypt. They think going to church or saying prayers, reading the Bible, or just believing in God is serving Him and is quite enough religion. But the service God required was in Canaan, in a different dimension altogether. He is not interested in our practicing religion, but rather in our finding reality in religion.

In other words, if we haven't accepted God's way of escape from Satan through Christ, it doesn't matter how many times we go to church or do religious things; we cannot please God! God told Pharaoh that His people needed to be free from Pharaoh's jurisdiction and released to offer acceptable sacrifices in another place altogether (Exodus 3:18). But the Lord "hardened Pharaoh's heart," and the ruler of Egypt wouldn't let the Israelites go out of his country (Exodus 10:20). Pharaoh was doing the Devil's work for him! It is always a very dangerous thing to do to harden your heart. If you harden it long enough and often enough, God will harden it for you in the end. He will give it a fixed setting.

So God began to make natural phenomena behave in an unusual way. If we won't pay attention to the still, small voice of the Spirit of God that insists that God is worth listening to, then God has to use a megaphone. This He did in the book of Exodus. He used polluted water, famine, corrupted crops, ecology, sickness, and death. Still Pharaoh hardened his heart. The same situation exists today. People can be like Pharaoh and not respond to God because of their adverse circumstances.

The plagues that God allows to come into our lives can result in either deliverance or defiance. People react in totally opposite ways to the troubles that God allows in our lives. John made a comment about this in Revelation 16:9, concerning the plagues that are predicted to trouble those on earth in the last days. "They were seared by the intense heat and they cursed the name of God, who had control over these plagues, but they refused to repent and glorify him." In verses 10–11, the writer stated that the people suffering from another God-permitted plague "gnawed their tongues in agony and cursed the God of heaven because of their pains and their sores."

The plagues that God allowed to affect the Egyptians resulted in a reaction of defiance. Actually, the king of Egypt acted like many of us do. While the plague was oppressing him, he softened; but when respite came, he hardened his heart. That sort of behavior isn't too different from ours or from that of some unbelievers I know.

It wasn't that Pharaoh and his servants weren't convinced God was speaking to them either. "This is the finger of God," his magicians exclaimed after Moses' rod swallowed up theirs (Exodus 8:19). Everyone recognized the power of Satan, and even the unbelievers recognized that the power of God was greater. Yet they continued to defy Him.

NOMINAL CHRISTIANITY

The people in Egypt who really wanted to believe in God and His promises, on the other hand, began to see the finger of God and hear the voice of God in the awful happenings around them. Those who were about to be delivered began to dare to look up, for their redemption was near. They were ready. At last, they recognized Moses as God's spokesman and experienced the results of his prevailing prayer on their behalf. They even felt the tyrannical grip of Pharaoh loosen. But then Pharaoh began to bargain, as Pharaoh always will when his hand is forced.

The proposals that Pharaoh offered to the children of Israel are the same proposals Satan offers people today: "Be a nominal believer. Keep letting Satan, not God, rule your life. By all means, look like a Christian on Sundays, but be yourself when no one's looking!" Satan has to think up a proposal that will encourage his slaves to decide to stay in Egypt of their own free will. So Pharaoh told Moses and Aaron, "Go, sacrifice to your God here in the land" (v. 25). What Pharaoh was suggesting was, "Look like a real believer but don't act like one!" That reminds me of Paul's description of some people in his day: "having a form of godliness but denying its power" (2 Timothy 3:5 NKJV).

I was once asked to have a young girl stay in our home. She was only sixteen years of age, and her parents were nearly out of their minds because she was seeing a twice-married man who was still married! The man's wife was not aware of his affair, but the girl's parents had discovered the relationship and wanted to get her away from the situation for a time.

The parents of the girl, however, were not believers, and

they did not want their daughter to become overly religious. They attended church, but that was as far as their spirituality went. Yet they wanted their daughter set free from the particular taskmaster of promiscuity. So they said, "Please, Jill, have her live with you, but don't convert her to your faith or anything like that! We just want her to have enough religion to make her respectable." In other words: "Sacrifice in Egypt! Teach her to look like a Christian and behave a little like a real Christian, without leaving her sin behind and turning to Christ."

It's the same as the proposal of Pharaoh, for Satan knows that "if the Son sets you free, you will be free indeed" (John 8:36), because our sinful appetites will no longer control us. That means coming out of Egypt altogether, into a totally new experience. However, it doesn't work to pretend we are free when we are not. We have to face reality and walk away from the task-masters of sex, drugs, lies, or stealing, and start a whole new life.

DON'T GO TOO FAR

Having failed to get Moses to comply with his request, and after a horrible plague of flies that got his attention for a short while, Pharaoh suggested another idea with the same end in mind. "Stay in sight. Don't get too involved. You can leave, but you don't have to go very far away. Why not leave an escape route so you can come back and serve me if you don't like it out there?"

Pharaoh said, "I will let you go to offer sacrifices to the LORD your God in the wilderness, but you must not go very far" (Exodus 8:28). Now, that sounds familiar. Today, people say, "If you must get into all this extreme Christianity, don't go too far. Don't get fanatical. You don't need to go overboard with this religious thing. People will think you are weird, and you will lose all your friends!" That's a bit like a little boy who fell out of bed one night. When his mother asked him what had happened, he said, "I guess I stayed too near where I got in!" Exactly! Many people are tempted by Pharaoh to do just that—to stay too near where they get in. They decide not to go too far in their discoveries of the Christian faith walk. "Leave your options open," Satan suggests. "Stay in sight of the old life." But this will never work, for you can't even see Canaan— the land of freedom and blessing—from Egypt. You need to make the journey out of the lifestyle you have been living into a whole new world. Moses answered this as he had the previous proposals, saying, in essence: "The Lord God of the Hebrews says, 'Let my people go.'"

DON'T INVOLVE THE FAMILY

The next suggested compromise is recorded in Exodus 10:8–11. Pharaoh suggested that only the Hebrew men should go and leave their families behind. "Don't involve everyone," he essentially said. "If you have to go, then go, but don't take your loved ones along with you."

When people are on the verge of being rescued, one of Satan's suggestions is often to imply that the whole business could well cause real division in the family. "Maybe some of your loved ones won't want to go with you into your Christian 'promised land.' Then what will you do?" Satan may ask. "It's not fair to get into this without your family, and it's too hazardous to take them into the wilderness with you." In this way, he uses what may indeed happen in your family relationships to prevent you from going ahead yourself!

Jesus warned us that our families may not always understand us if we become Christians. We might even find ourselves facing the worst opposition from our own relatives. Jesus experienced such things Himself. But Jesus simply told His followers this is all part of being responsible for our own choices, and we need to take up our cross and follow Him (Luke 9:23). One of the hardest things in following Christ is to leave those you love behind you in the matter of faith!

After I became a Christian, it was very hard for me to share my newfound faith with my parents. I remember wondering if I could get a minister to visit our home and explain "the new me" to them. I was saying to myself, "Here am I, Lord . . . send the vicar!" I was scared that my parents wouldn't understand (which they didn't), that I would find an invisible wall rising between us (which I did), and that I would offend them (which happened!). "I'm the only one who has accepted Christ in my family," I moaned to a friend. "Maybe I should wait till they want to become Christians too."

"Don't say, 'I'm the only one,'" she responded cheerfully. "Say, 'I'm the first one'!" That helped, and I determined to share my new spiritual discoveries with my much-loved family whatever the reaction or result.

Moses told Pharaoh that God's will was for all the family to have the opportunity to go and worship Him, and it was the men's responsibility as the head of the family to see that they had the chance to do so.

Pharaoh had nearly finished fighting with words. With lice,

locusts, and frogs coming out of his ears, he made one desperate suggestion. "Go, worship the LORD. Even your women and children may go with you; only leave your flocks and herds behind" (Exodus 10:24).

But the cattle would be needed, and so would the goods. Moses insisted, "Our livestock too must go with us; not a hoof is to be left behind" (v. 26). All we have and are is needed to serve our God. Sacrificing to Jehovah involves everything. A Christian commitment is not merely spiritual; it is a lifestyle touching many aspects of everyday life. Our person *and* our possessions are involved.

THE WAY OUT

The contest was nearly over. Pharaoh's proposals had been rejected. It was time to escape, to be delivered. What was it going to take to make Pharaoh finally release the children of Israel? It would take the death of the firstborn.

Just as it would take the death of Pharaoh's firstborn to force him to set the people free, so, thousands of years later, the firstborn of God, Jesus Christ, would set the world of sin-slaves free. Obviously, Pharaoh did not want to let anyone go; but Jesus, in stark contrast, came to set men free. The death of Christ was prefigured in what happened next—the sacrificial lamb of Exodus, which would play a vital part in the people's redemption. The death of the lamb, a picture of the death of the beloved Son of God, would forever be part of Israel's heritage.

God is a God of justice, but God is also a God of love. In love God warns, and in love God commands. Love that lays no limits isn't love. And love's limits have been outraged by sinful man's trespasses so that God must judge, even though God also must love.

The dilemma of a just God who is love was solved when He told His people in Egypt, "Take a lamb" (Exodus 12:3). The pattern was set. The Israelites who would be delivered were to take a lamb without defect and kill it. Then they were to put the blood of the animal on the doorposts of their houses so that when the angel of death passed over their homes and families, he would "pass over" those who sheltered under the blood (vv. 1–11).

These people had no way of knowing the eternal significance of the instructions they were given. But as they obeyed and kept the Passover in succeeding generations, this action picture of our redemption spoke louder than words could ever have done. The lamb, without defect, spoke of the Lord Jesus, "the Lamb of God, who takes away the sin of the world" (John 1:29). The little lamb, kept four long days under scrutiny to validate its perfection, proved to the children of Israel its innocence and was a vivid picture of Jesus Christ, who was kept under the hostile scrutiny of his enemies and was able to inquire of them, "Can any of you prove me guilty of sin?" (John 8:46). None could accuse Jesus, for God's Lamb was indeed perfect, without defect.

The lamb of the Exodus Passover had to be one year old. The age of innocence with the nature of meekness, beautifully prefiguring God's own special Sacrifice, who was "led like a lamb to the slaughter, and as a sheep before her shearers is silent, so he did not open his mouth" (Isaiah 53:7).

The lamb of the Exodus Passover had to be killed in the evening at the ninth hour, and we are told in Matthew 27:46, "About the ninth hour Jesus cried out with a loud voice . . . 'My

God, my God, why have you forsaken me?'" (ESV). Having killed the lamb at the ninth hour, the people in Egypt then had to apply the blood to the doorposts of their homes. In Leviticus 17:11 we are told that life is in the blood, and Hebrews 9:22 states that "without the shedding of blood there is no forgiveness [of sin]." By a life given, there was to be deliverance from judgment.

"Christ, our Passover lamb" was sacrificed for us two thousand years ago (1 Corinthians 5:7), and if we personally apply the merits of His lifeblood poured out for our sins, the God of justice will pass over us! (See Exodus 12:13.) Jesus Christ is "the Lamb who was slain" for you and me personally "from the creation of the world" (Revelation 13:8).

And so, one dark night in Egypt, the time arrived. Death came in judgment to every home without the blood of a Passover lamb upon its doorposts. Terrible cries of agony ascended into the darkened skies, and Pharaoh—in whose palace all the firstborn died, including his own son—finally let the children of Israel go. It took the death of his child for Pharaoh to loosen his evil grip.

A TASTE OF FREEDOM

The people were well ready. They had been told to eat the Passover meal in haste, ready for flight. When the time came, we read that they went out in one big dash. They just took off, glad to be free, thrilled to be rid of Pharaoh's land and his taskmasters' whips. Their excitement and joy knew no bounds. A sort of euphoria gripped them. The visible presence of God was right there with them. His presence was manifested in a cloud during the day and a pillar of fire at night. What a fantastic experience that must have been! Everyone was involved. Talking and chattering, they shared their stories of deliverance. The fellowship was good, God was good, and everything else was good. No giants, no problems, just a heady taste of freedom.

Having "spoiled" the Egyptians, the Israelites were rich beyond their wildest dreams. They showed each other the good garments, the gold and silver and precious jewels that their enemies had pressed upon them in their desperation to get rid of them (Exodus 12:35–36). What an exhilarating time!

Let us pause here. Does this mirror your experience of redemption? Do you remember the day you accepted Jesus as your deliverer, claiming His death on your behalf? Do you recollect the leap you took from all that was familiar, into the new and exciting unknown? Can you picture again the happy fellowship as you began to travel along the road to freedom with others of like mind? Do you remember sharing your story with them? And do you recollect the joy of finding yourself the possessor of unbelievable spiritual riches: peace of mind and the joy of forgiveness—in fact, all the spiritual riches that are in Christ? Do you remember?

Do you remember the visible sense of God with you, as real as that cloud or pillar of fire? Didn't you feel you could almost touch Him? Why, you believed you were ready for *anything!*

But then, suddenly the whole scene changed. The Red Sea loomed ahead—an impossible barrier to all the children of Israel. They realized that there had been a strange sort of security in slavery. Fears swept away the happy feelings that had filled their hearts in those first few glorious days or weeks of liberty, and they even voiced such sentiments such as, "It was better in Egypt!"

This is quite a usual thing to happen to young Christians.

You see, almost immediately after you have been set free from slavery to sin, "Pharaoh" begins to pursue you. Enraged at your escape, he takes his army and his taskmasters and begins to chase you. Distance always lends enchantment to the view, and suddenly slavery can seem a good, safe way of life. The euphoria fades quickly away and there you are, facing the Red Sea.

"Oh God, here I am," you cry. "I'm between the Devil and the deep Red Sea. I can't go on, and I can't go back. The future looks impassable and the present impossible."

You actually can become very angry. Angry at "Moses," whoever he or she happens to be. Who shared with you this message of deliverance in the first place? Who brought you out of your bondage and security to live in this unsafe wilderness (Exodus 14:11)?

I remember being back at college, after my stay in the hospital where I had been converted to Christ, finding sudden disappointments as intimidating as the Red Sea barring my way forward in my Christian walk. My old friends didn't understand my religious enthusiasm—"fanaticism," they called it! My drama teacher gave me a failing grade on my recitation exam because I suddenly refused to say all the foul words the script demanded. (Leaving them out made nonsense of the script, which my teacher didn't appreciate!) My roommate didn't like my new habits of prayer and Bible reading late at night when she wanted to sleep and I had the bed light on. Even my professors addressed what they perceived as "an unbalanced view of religion, leading to odd behavior patterns, not conducive to the common good"!

I began to grumble against "Moses." Why hadn't "my Moses," Jenny, warned me how difficult living a Christian life would be? She should have told me I could get into serious trouble! The funny thing was, I had been getting into trouble for being bad; now I was getting into trouble for being good! And like the children of Israel, I was having second thoughts.

All this, I discovered, is quite normal, so take heart if it is happening to you. Moses can't be expected to tell you all that you will possibly meet as you set out on the Christian life. Moses himself didn't know all the problems that lay ahead, but he stuck with his people throughout the entire experience. Your "Moses" will stick with you if he or she is any sort of spiritual parent at all, and together you will sink or swim through your Red Sea. You might even walk right through it together on dry ground.

The thing to do is to think back carefully and realistically to your position before you came to faith and realize it was not really better in Egypt. Anything has to be better than that! And the fact that Pharaoh is pursuing you does not mean he can catch you, and however scary his soldiers sound as they pound up behind you, God promises that His presence is with you.

GO FORWARD

The cloud in Exodus 14 was the visible manifestation of the invisible God. You and I have to learn to look through the cloud at Pharaoh, by faith. This way you will get a right assessment of his size. He will certainly be diminished when you filter him that way. God promises in Romans 6:14 that "sin shall no longer be your master." Sin might look fierce, and it might make all sorts of noises, but God has promised that sin need not be your taskmaster once you are delivered out of Egypt. Stand still, and stop jumping up and down in anger about the person or church that got you into all this, and instead learn to see the salvation of the Lord (Exodus 14:13).

"The LORD will fight for you," Moses assured the people (v. 14), and as God protects you from the Enemy who is already a defeated foe, He will quietly reassure you that He is with you and that you need to listen to some instructions and obey.

When you face these first obstacles in your new life in Christ and there seems no way through them or around them—in fact, the barrier seems just as deep and wide and impassable as the Red Sea was to the children of Israel—then listen to God's command: "Tell the Israelites to move on" (v. 15). In other words, go forward! As you obey this seemingly impossible command and refuse to go back, you will find the waters will divide and you will go through safely on dry ground. It's a question of faith, not feelings. A Red Sea experience is one every newly born-again Christian has to face.

The wonderful feelings of your immediate escape will surely diminish, and doubts of all sorts and sizes will set in. "What have I let myself in for? I didn't think I would face this. They never told me that!" you will say. But go forward. Obey God's Word without considering those frightened feelings, and you will find that Pharaoh and all his army will be drowned in the very area where he had hoped to see your defeat.

So you are delivered but find yourself between the Devil and the deep Red Sea? Then go forward, right through it, and you will find yourself safely on the other side of your first big test. Then perhaps you will sing a song of victory like the one recorded in Exodus 15!

It's time to discover, discuss, and then apply the discoveries you have made. If you are using this for your own study time, record your findings in a notebook.

Summary

In a sentence or two, summarize what this chapter is about.

Discovery

Review what the following characters and things can be said to represent:

Pharaoh

Moses

The plagues

The Passover lamb

The treasures of Egypt

The pillar of cloud and fire

The deep Red Sea

Discussion or Journal

1. Working in pairs within your group, or alone in your journal, look up and discuss some further scriptures that deal with the proposals of Pharaoh as they were used by Satan to prevent people from being delivered. Here are some examples:

   a. *Sacrifice in bondage.* Nominal Christianity; giving God unacceptable sacrifices (1 Peter 1:18–19).

    b. *Stay in sight.* Don't fully commit yourself
      (Romans 12:1–2).

    c. *Spare your families.* Don't offend your family
      with your faith (Luke 8:19–21; Matthew 10:34–38;
      Luke 9:59–62).

    d. *Leave the cattle.* Let it be a spiritual thing,
      not a practical one (Exodus 20:24–25; 31:1–11;
      35:4–29). What were the goods to be used for?

2. Read John 1:29, which reminds us of Jesus as the
   Lamb who has been prefigured in the Passover.
   Discuss what John the Baptist's words would
   mean to his audience. What can they mean to us?

Decision

1. What in this chapter most applies to you?
2. What do you need to do about it?

Devotion

1. Pray about the discoveries you made while
   reading this chapter.
2. Pray for your family and friends who don't
   understand the changes they see in you. Ask God
   to help you take them with you into the "promised
   land."

A Personal Spiritual Workout

1. Turn to the victory song of Moses in Exodus 15:1–19.

    a. Read it through to yourself.

    b. Moses sang in triumph about three things the Lord was to him personally (v. 2). What are they?

    c. Gather the attributes of God that Moses spoke of from the following verses, and make a list of them: verses 3, 6, 7, 11, 13, 18.

    d. What should be the result of the news of the people's deliverance on those who hear about it? (vv. 14–16)

2. Write a note in your journal about the lesson you learned.

FIVE

THE OTHER SIDE
OF REDEMPTION

The children of Israel had run away from their past and had started running toward their future.

They sang songs, cried, and laughed all at once, while the children stayed close to their parents' sides and hurried toward a mysterious world ahead of them that they knew absolutely nothing about. They were all on "the other side of redemption."

It was exciting—for a while. Then reality set in. After the euphoria of the escape, mothers began to worry if they had brought enough food for the journey. Of course they had no idea how long they would be on the road. *It could be a week, or it could be a month or a year,* some of them must have thought to themselves. Well, they had brought all their livestock with them, so they had plenty of meat for a long while; and they had unleavened bread and water in the waterskins for the immediate future.

Then the cloud and the pillar of fire came, shining the way at night and protecting them from the pursuing soldiers during the day. But nothing could have prepared them for the vast expanse of the water in front of them and the ominous sound of the pursuing horsemen behind them.

And then Moses held up his rod and shouted, "Move on! Go forward!" *Where to?* the people must have wondered. Surely Moses couldn't expect them to simply walk forward into the sea and drown! But then the sea parted right in front of their feet, standing up on each side like two mighty walls. It was a miracle! And the vast multitude walked through the middle of the Red Sea with their hearts in their mouths and hope in their hearts. They surely dared not breathe lest the waters close over their heads. So they were saved from the Egyptians.

What a sobering sight it must have been to watch the pursuing army racing for their lives for dry land and see them disappear with desperate cries under the returning waters of the sea! Once safely through themselves, Miriam led the children of Israel in a celebration of worship and dancing. "Both horse and driver he has hurled into the sea," she sang. "The LORD is my strength and my defense; he has become my salvation" (Exodus 15:1–2). There the people camped, and there they reveled in God—for a while.

SAVED, SATISFIED, AND STUCK

Delivered! But why? What was next? To be sure, God did not intend his redeemed people to live forever on the Red Sea shore. Many of us come to faith and "camp" on the decision, as it were, forever. We can be tempted to decide that joining the church, being baptized, or even walking the aisle at the conclusion of an evangelistic meeting is the beginning and end of all that is necessary.

The children of Israel could well have been happy with this state of affairs. Their victory had indeed been a great one, and the temptation was to stay and sing about it forever. But on the other side of the Red Sea, God instructed Moses to tell the people to go forward. He had not meant them to go forward only to the other side of the problem. I am quite sure He meant them to go forward *ad infinitum*. To keep going forward day after day and year after year.

The Christian life is all about going forward, going on. The journey of faith is not a step, a leap, or even a plunge through the Red Sea. It is supposed to be a steady, daily walking along the path of God for your life. One of the problems is we don't know this. Another problem is we run out of gas!

One day, my husband took up racquetball. Knowing I needed the exercise, I also ventured into the little box that was the court. It seemed a trifle small for the two of us, but it was fun. Having played tennis years ago, in the days of my youth, I managed quite well. However, being thoroughly out of shape, I found myself running furiously in every direction for about twenty minutes and then suddenly collapsing in a whimpering heap in a corner of the court.

My experience reminded me of many young Christians. Starting off with great enthusiasm, they leap frantically around, chasing the ball and running themselves into the ground, ending up out of breath and beaten in a short span of time. This is not the way to play the game. Watch an expert racquetball player, and you see he paces himself well, knowing just where to put his feet. He even finishes a vigorous game with steps left over. The idea is to plod with God, rather than to race through space!

Sitting exhausted in a hotel chair, American pastor Vance Havner was asked by a lady in his group if he was enjoying his tour of Jerusalem. He replied, "Madam, I am exhausted. Today I ran where Jesus walked!" Those of us who have been on such tours understand how he felt. But you know, we are not intended to "run where Jesus walked." We are to walk with steady, measured tread in the steps of the Master.

This was undoubtedly what God had in mind for His children after their incredible rescue from Egypt. Now their new life could begin. It was not on God's agenda for them to be saved, satisfied, and stuck on the other side of redemption!

Would you say you are saved, satisfied, and stuck? Are you standing on the other side of redemption wondering what to do with your newfound freedom? Do you want to settle for pitching a tent and settling down to a lifetime of mediocrity? Don't miss out on all that's ahead! Stay healthy, exercise to stay in shape, and take warning from what happened to the children of Israel!

THE "G VIRUS"

Almost immediately after crossing the Red Sea, the Israelites all got sick. They all caught a deadly virus. It was far more virulent and lethal than any virus we are familiar with that brings death and destruction to our world. It was the G virus—the "grumble" germ—and it threatened to stop the whole plan of redemption in its tracks! All but two occurrences of "grumbling" in the Old Testament are found in six chapters of the Pentateuch: Exodus 15, 16, and 17, and Numbers 14, 16, and 17. Of all the sins of the fathers, God counted this one of the worst. It is one of Satan's most effective weapons because it robs us of God and robs God of us!

Sometimes learning what God thinks about our grumbles helps us to deal with them. First of all, God hears us when we gripe and grumble. Numbers 11:18 says, "The LORD heard you when you wailed." Over and over again the Bible says that God heard the Israelites' griping and their grumbling. We need to know that God doesn't want to hear it!

Our son and daughter-in-law have seven children. There is a sign displayed in a prominent place in their kitchen that says briefly and succinctly: "No whining!" Whining is unacceptable behavior to those parents, and it is unacceptable to God. It poisons the environment and spoils relationships.

It makes God sad to hear us whine, and it also makes Him mad! "Now the people complained about their hardships in the hearing of the LORD, and when he heard them his anger was aroused" (v. 1). God wants us to know that wailing and whining are unacceptable behaviors.

The Israelites were on their way to the promised land. They were going to possess their possessions and inherit their inheritance! Canaan represents, for Christians, the place God has chosen for us on this earth. It is not a physical place, but a spiritual position. This spiritual position, or plane of experience, can be called the overcoming Christian life.

We need to figure out what God has in mind for us as soon as possible after we have received Jesus. Only a few days away from your experience of conversion you need to understand two things. First, you need to grasp what has already happened to you, and second, you need to understand what should happen next.

FALLING DOWN

When you received Christ by His Spirit, He entered your heart and brought forgiveness with Him (Colossians 1:14). He made you a whole new person inside and gave you a whole new start (2 Corinthians 5:17). He promised you that He would never abandon you or throw you away (John 6:37). You are like a penny standing upright in the palm of His nail-pierced hand. You may fall down, but you can never fall out. The penny is so small, but the hand of the One who loves you is so large. You are His and He is yours. It's a sort of "exchanged life," as Christian missionary Hudson Taylor once described it. You get Christ and He gets you. To be sure, He gets the raw end of the deal, but never mind, that is all grace!

Have you fallen down? Have you dishonored the Lord? Have you betrayed Him, refused to obey Him, resisted Him, or ignored Him? Have you grumbled about Him? Have you even wondered if you have fallen away from God, fallen out of His hand? Well, remember, you will fall down—as we all do— but you can never fall out. "No one can snatch [you] out of my Father's hand," promised Jesus (John 10:29).

You need to start moving forward. It's important to know what to do next, once you have said that vital prayer of commitment. Becoming a Christian is easy, but being a Christian day by day by day is another thing altogether. The exciting possibility is this: It's entirely up to you how long it takes before you start living in the good of all that God has in mind for you. It is also up to you to get into God's Word, find out what you're supposed to do, and then do it.

The route from the Red Sea into the land of Canaan probably should have taken the children of Israel a few months. Instead, it took them forty years, and the generation that escaped from Egypt never did make it in. They spent forty years going around in circles in the wilderness, simply because of initial starting problems. And one of those problems was grumbling.

We shall not make the journey of faith without falling down on the job, but we shall make it, God willing, if we keep our eyes on Jesus! Whatever the sin that may take us down on the way, we must make sure we are never counted out.

THE FINE ART OF MOVING ON

I see clearly, looking back on my own experience, how very fortunate I was to have a "Moses" to help me. The girl who led me to Jesus Christ instructed me clearly and concisely on the art of moving on. She did not allow me to be saved, satisfied, and stuck! She showed me how to pray, read the Word, witness, and worship, and she provided me with friendship and fellowship along the way. God blessed me with Jenny's love and spiritual oversight, and this initial mentoring was very special and important to me. She invested in my life. She took the time and trouble to take me to the next level. She insisted I could make it to the promised land, and she prayed me up when I was down, was calm when I was confused, and was fresh when I was frantic. I owe her so very, very much.

It's important that, if possible, you find a spiritually mature person to help you on your way. Find someone who loves the Lord and His Word and will answer all the questions you are bound to need answered. I hung on every word Jenny spoke to me. I came to respect her and soon had her on a pedestal, certainly not of her choosing. This is very normal too. We tend to be "people worshipers" anyway, and when someone has been a help in the spiritual area of our lives, what better person to idolize?

But one thing I didn't know was that this is not allowed. God says, "You shall have no other gods before me" (Exodus 20:3). It is very important that we keep our spiritual leaders in perspective. We must neither place them on pedestals nor worship them in any form. This does not mean we do not appreciate, pray for, respect, and listen to them. We should obey their direction if they are our human shepherds, but we must not place any person in God's place. The pedestal is reserved for Jehovah God, who alone is to be worshipped. After all, we are only models of growth and learning, not models of perfection!

The first bad experience the children of Israel had in their walk toward Canaan concerned this very issue. Moses fell off his pedestal. Placed on it by the ecstatic people, he managed to keep this elevated position in their affections for precisely three days. Then he fell off into a sand dune, and the trouble began (Exodus 15:22–27).

Moses had his first tussle with the crowd when they saw Pharaoh's army marching after them. "Was it because there were no graves in Egypt that you brought us to the desert to die? What have you done to us by bringing us out of Egypt? . . . It would have been better for us to serve the Egyptians than to die in the desert," they grumbled (Exodus 14:11–12).

THE WATERS OF BITTERNESS

"When they came to Marah, they could not drink its water because it was bitter. (That is why the place is called Marah.) So the people grumbled against Moses, saying, 'What are we to drink?'" (Exodus 15:23–24).

Israel's first stop is traditionally placed by the local Arabs at Ain Musa, the Springs of Moses, a site not mentioned in any biblical text. It was apparently a source of sweet water about sixteen to eighteen hours' journey north of the site connected with Marah (which means "bitter"), Israel's first-mentioned stop. The journey from Ain Musa to Marah was about forty miles. That doesn't sound like much unless you are walking through deep, white, glaring sand in the Middle Eastern sun along with the entire extended family of all ages and sizes, plus all your animals—and you run out of water! You can imagine the Israelites' shouts of joy when the springs came into sight.

The dash to fill up the waterskins began—but the people's cries of joy changed to howls of disappointment as they discovered that the waters were brackish, horribly bitter, and according to tradition, very salty. That's all you need—salt water in the desert sun! I can imagine Moses and Aaron and Miriam looking at each other in consternation, knowing there was no way to travel further without life-saving water to drink.

The grumbling began. The people forgot all about the miracles of the plagues in Egypt and their incredible rescue at the Red Sea. They turned to Moses and demanded water to drink.

God showed Moses a tree, a branch of which he threw into the water, and the waters were sweetened (healed) and made fit to drink. For a while, a very short while, Moses was back in favor with the people again. This was the first of many tests to show the children of Israel that they needed to trust God and not man. As the hymn writer says:

> *I dare not trust the sweetest frame,*
> *But wholly lean on Jesus' name!*[1]

I remember the day that Jenny (the girl who led me to Christ) fell off the pedestal on which I had placed her. It was as bitter an experience for me as the waters of Marah were for the children of Israel. I was angry and upset, simply because I had come to depend on her and she let me down. It was not Jenny's fault. She had never told me to depend on anyone but Jesus, but when you are a young Christian that's hard. It's so much easier to depend on "the holy person" rather than on the Holy Spirit!

Relying on a person instead of on God can be a serious thing, though. As we look at the incident in the book of Exodus, we see that the loss of the people's confidence and respect in their human leadership led quite naturally to a loss of confidence in God. That is indeed serious. People will always disappoint you, even someone as wonderful as Moses (or Jenny). Then what will happen to your confidence in God?

Perhaps this has happened to you. You trusted a Christian friend or leader and then found out he or she was not perfect, as you secretly thought. Perhaps he lost his temper or bawled you out or didn't tell you the truth. Maybe she wasn't up front with you and promised you something she couldn't deliver. Did you get angry with that person, grumble about him or her to others, and then transfer that anger to God? The problem is that you are watching a leader learning to lead. No human authority is perfect. This does not lessen that person's authority, but we must realize that our spiritual leaders are learning, just like we are.

OH, I NEVER EXPECTED THIS!

I edit *Just Between Us,* a magazine for women who are wives of pastors and missionaries, and women who love the Lord and want to serve Him in their churches.[2] Every so often I ask veteran leaders, "What nearly 'did you in' as you grew in your new faith as a leader?" They reply, "I was shattered by the way veteran Christians around me treated each other. It nearly caused me to quit the church. Oh, I never expected this!"

Somehow we expect more of our Christian leaders, and we can become very discouraged when, around the corner of our glad, "Yes, Lord! I will go anywhere You want me to go and do anything You ask me to do, with whomever You ask me to do it," we find ourselves disillusioned by the less-than-Christlike behavior of those with whom we serve. To be fair, our expectations are usually far too high. Maybe you have had unfair expectations of your leaders. Have you been bitterly disappointed and felt let down? We need to give them some slack sometimes.

Moses, for example, hadn't had much practice leading. Well, certainly, not leading thousands of people through a desert. Every minute these grumbling, mumbling followers seemed to be saying to him, "You didn't tell us it would be like this!" Moses could easily have answered, "I didn't know! And if I had have known, I might have left you behind in Egypt! I never expected this!"

Just think of Moses' problem. Here he was, with thousands of thirsty people on his hands. I wonder if he thought back to his loyal flock of sheep and goats in the wilderness. At least they didn't answer him back! They trusted their human shepherd to do the very best for them. It wasn't fair. Why were these people expecting him to provide water? Why did they look at him as if he were a waterfall deliberately damming up the flow?

It is never fair to expect our leaders to supply what God alone can give us. That is not their job. Their job is simply to direct us to our source of supply and satisfaction—the Holy Spirit—and instruct us in how to drink. Sometimes we lean on our leaders or, if we are married, even on our spouses to be our Holy Spirit. That's not fair!

There is nothing that gets to Stuart and me more, in our positions of leadership, than to have our motives suspected. To be met with suspicious mistrust when we are doing our level, albeit imperfect, best is a very depressing thing. Also trying to live up to a bar that has been raised too high, or even making genuine mistakes and not being given another chance, is really discouraging. It is not only a bitter experience for followers to see their leader fail to produce; it is also a bitter thing for a leader to have his motives misunderstood and be expected to do the impossible, which only God can do.

THE LORD SHOWED HIM A TREE

C. I. Scofield wrote, "These bitter waters [of Marah] were in the very path of the Lord's leading, and stand for the trials of God's people, which are educatory and not punitive. The 'tree' which healed the waters, should remind the Christian that the Cross, which became sweet to Christ as the expression of the Father's will can take the bitterness out of all such experiences. When we accept our Marahs, we cast the 'tree' into the waters and blessing and growth follow."[3]

Moses knew how to make the bitter waters better. The Lord showed him a tree. That's what He always does for me whenever I am on my knees complaining about people complaining. God shows me a tree. He shows me Jesus hanging on it, and I see He's not saying anything at all, except little sentences like, "Father, forgive them," or, "They know not what they do," or, "I thirst." That last one usually gets to me. The Son of God thirsted not only for moisture in His torture of crucifixion, but for the souls of the men and women He died to save. "What shall I drink, Father?" Jesus cried upon the cross. "The bitter waters of Marah," was the reply. The cup of suffering and death! And He drank from that cup, with never a complaint.

Because of Christ's obedience, we can apply the tree that God shows us in the Bible, the cross of our Lord Jesus Christ, to our bitterness and have it turned into a sweet experience instead. The Lord will show you a tree, and as you apply the cross to your bitter waters, there will be a healing (Exodus 15:25). The G virus has to be healed. The medicine for grumbling and complaining for both leader and follower is a tree.

The Bible says that all this happened to test them (v. 25). What was the test? The test was to see if they would depend on Him instead of Moses and Aaron. It was not punitive, but rather educational. The test was to prove what was deep down in their hearts. To see if the deadly virus of discontent and rebellion was lurking in the soul. God took their temperature at regular intervals to find out if they would love and obey Him.

TAKING OUR SPIRITUAL
TEMPERATURE

Years ago, we visited Singapore. As we came off the elevator into the arrival hall, we were invited to step through a booth set up to take our temperature. You simply walked through a metal door-like structure, which somehow determined if your temperature was elevated. The dreaded SARS virus was frightening everyone! That very morning, a man suspected of testing positive for the virus was put in isolation in a hospital. It was in the morning papers.

We were told how incredibly swiftly the disease spread and how deadly the disease was. No one wanted to catch it, and no one wanted to carry it! As we moved around Singapore, we saw warnings everywhere not to touch door handles, to be considerate of others and keep washing our hands, and more. Oh, that we believers were as cautious and careful about the G virus as we are about the SARS virus! Perhaps we need to be educated about the virulent nature of grumbling.

As we arrive in a new situation each day, we should allow God to take our spiritual temperature. We should take every precaution for our own well-being, for our loved ones' sake, and for the good of the community as a whole. Get checked out and try to stop the disease of sin in its early stages. God forbid we should contract the wretched thing, but if we do, we need to remember, there is a tree!

All this does not mean we have scriptural permission to throw off all earthly authority and be spiritual mavericks. Our place is under the authority of godly leadership and oversight. But, under that God-given delegated authority, we are supposed to grow and become supportive and helpful to that very leadership placed over us. This is the way to spiritual health: to listen and obey God through His appointed leadership, to grow up so fast we can easily discern our leaders' mistakes, and to pray for, support, and respect our leaders.

AFTER MARAH COMES ELIM

After Marah came the oasis of Elim (v. 27). Elim was a welcomed sight as the whole nation rounded the white-hot sand dunes and saw the oasis glistening before them with its long grasses and tamarisk trees and an abundance of water. Twelve sweet wells of water were found there, one for each tribe, representing complete sufficiency for everyone's needs. Seventy palm trees provided shade from the heat and gave them rest from their marching.

The psalmist wrote, "Weeping may stay for the night, but rejoicing comes in the morning" (Psalm 30:5). It was finally time for respite. Jesus was tempted by the Devil forty days, and afterward the angels came (Matthew 4:11). Elijah, exhausted, ran away from the queen Jezebel, who sought his life. After he could run no more, the angel of the Lord appeared, strengthening him (1 Kings 19:7). After Marah, God will always provide an Elim, a place of spiritual rest and refreshment in the middle of your desert. After Marah comes Elim—don't forget it.

Part of growing in God and in the knowledge of our Lord Jesus Christ is to look past the Marahs of our lives to the Elims on the horizon. There will be a better day around the corner of our trials and testing. This hope is what will help us past hurdles and is the way we learn to walk by faith.

A child clings to his father's hand as he takes his first tottering steps forward. In love, the father must remove his hand so that the child may walk alone. What a ludicrous sight it would be to see a grown man clinging to his father's hand. Yet how many people, having been Christians for years, have never yet let go and learned to walk as God intended them to walk? They cling, metaphorically speaking, to their pastor's hand. They leave their physical babies in the nursery, yet they are spiritual babies themselves. In the same way, the child who begins to walk on his own begins to drink on his own. No longer does he demand that his father hold the cup to his thirsty lips. The little hands take the cup for themselves and lift the drink to the lips. The child is surely still dependent on his father to provide the drink, but he is growing up enough to appropriate the liquid for himself.

So go forward to Elim. Find your well and your palm tree. Take a rest and a drink that has been provided by your loving heavenly Father. Camp there for a while, but don't stay too long. Remember, you are not intended to wander around in circles, getting nowhere for forty years. You are intended to march into the promised land. How long will it take you? It depends entirely on which route you take. Listen to and obey the One who drew up the plan and sketched out the way, and you'll pass through the dry desert and soon arrive in Canaan!

It's time to discover, discuss, and then apply the discoveries you have made. If you are using this for your own study time, record your findings in a notebook.

Summary

In a sentence or two, summarize what this chapter is about.

Discovery

1. Which part of this chapter was meaningful and why? Share with the group or write a sentence or two about it.
2. What do you think about putting people on pedestals?
3. Share a Marah/Elim experience.

Discussion or Journal

1. The Bible has a lot to say about the life of a Christian. Look up the following verses and paraphrase each in your own words.

   a. Romans 6:4
   b. Ephesians 5:2
   c. Romans 8:1, 4
   d. Ephesians 5:15
   e. Romans 13:13
   f. Colossians 2:6

2. The Bible has a lot to say about authority. Who gives the rulers of the world authority?
   a. Read Daniel 2:20–21, 37, 44.
   b. Read Daniel's interpretation of Nebuchadnezzar's nightmare in Daniel 4:19–37. Write down your deductions from this passage about God giving man authority to rule.

3. What does the Bible say about believers being subject to authority, and what authorities does it talk about? Read the following verses in reference to this:

   a. Ephesians 5:24

   b. 1 Peter 5:5

   c. James 4:7

   d. 1 Timothy 3-4

   e. Romans 13:1

   f. 1 Peter 3:1, 5

   g. Titus 3:1

   h. 1 Corinthians 16:16

   i. 1 Peter 2:18

   j. 1 Peter 2:13-14

4. Remember: When the law of man contravenes the law of God, we ought to obey God rather than man! Discuss.

Decision

1. What in this chapter most applies to you?
2. What do you need to do about it?

Devotion

1. Take one or two of these verses about the walk of faith each day and memorize it.
   a) 1 Corinthians 3:3
   b) Colossians 4:5
   c) 2 Corinthians 4:2

d) 1 Thessalonians 3:6

e) Ephesians 2:10

f) 1 John 1:6

g) Ephesians 4:1

h) 1 John 1:7

i) 3 John 4

A Personal Spiritual Workout

Each day choose a thought or look up a verse or your notes pertaining to the lessons learned and *meditate* (which means to "chew it over") throughout the day. Pray about it each night.

SIX

MANNA IN THE MORNING

The children of Israel had sand in their sandwiches, a monotonous landscape, thirsty children, and bickering families! There were no supermarkets or corner grocery stores in the desert. And now there was no bread! I can't say I blame them for their complaints (Exodus 16:1–8).

God was testing them, and they continued to fail the test (v. 3). Not only were they grumbling and griping, but they were looking back. That's a dangerous preoccupation. Like Lot's wife, you stand the chance of being turned into a pillar of salt!

DON'T LOOK BACK

Lot's wife wanted to be back in Sodom; the children of Israel wanted to be back in Egypt. "Would to God we were back in Egypt. There was plenty to eat there," they whined. "Egypt is a great place to die. Why have you brought us out here to deliberately kill us with hunger?"

Moses answered them, "You are not grumbling against us, but against the LORD" (v. 8).

That comment should give us pause to ponder. Our complaining is against God! If God has brought us to Himself, we can't look back, only forward. We must put our hand to the plow and stay focused or we will not plow a straight furrow.

Are you looking back? Perhaps you are missing Egypt. There was perhaps a measure of security in serving Pharaoh. Now you aren't sure what's ahead. Life isn't a rose garden, and for the Christian things can get sticky! But it is important when trouble comes not to look back. If you spend your time sighing and crying and playing the "if only" game, you will find yourself turning around and returning to Egypt!

As I began to witness to my friends after my conversion to Christ, I discovered my new beliefs were affecting my friendships. An unseen barrier had come between us. It was horrible. I realized my new lifestyle was putting them in an awkward position. I couldn't participate anymore in the risqué parties, the easy half-truths and downright lying that had been part of my life, or the bad language and blasphemy that had so easily rolled off my tongue before Jesus came into my heart. This made my friends feel as if I had adopted a holier-than-thou attitude. It also made them uncomfortable doing the things they had felt perfectly comfortable doing before!

Our friendships came under considerable strain, and I faced the real possibility that I could lose all my friends. Then I did lose them! At that point I sat alone in my college dormitory and said somewhat bitterly, "I want to go back to Egypt! I'm 'hungry' for my friends!" I began to grumble about the situation, first under my breath and then to my "Moses," Jenny.

Jenny merely gave me a long, hard look and commented on the fact that Jesus lost all His friends for me—in fact, one betrayed Him, one denied Him, and the rest abandoned Him! "Anyway, Jill," she said cheerfully, "what sort of friends are they if they leave you because you have found a faith that works and a God who is real? God will give you more friends!" And that was the end of my little rebellion. I wanted to object, "But I don't want new friends, I want my old familiar ones back," but I knew deep inside it would never happen unless they came to know Jesus too.

I told Jesus that I was so sorry I had looked back and had very nearly gone back and that I wanted to go forward now, however the friend issue turned out. I put myself under Jenny's oversight again, packed up my tent, and took off into the wild blue yonder for Jesus Christ. Don't look back—or go back even in your thoughts. Discipline your mind not to go there!

Most of the complaints of the people of God as they tramped through the hard places of the desert were quite understandable. There was no water and there was no bread. You can't live without either, so they had some good grounds for grumbling. The mistake they made was to get after Moses and Aaron instead of going straight to the Lord! That was my mistake too. I learned to turn straight to the Lord as soon as I found myself tempted to think about Egypt.

If only we would learn, at the start of our spiritual journey, to take our complaint straight to the complaint department.

Notice where that is: It is not the pastor's office (Moses' tent) or an Egyptian friend. It is the Lord Himself we need to talk to. He is the One who hears our grumbling anyway, and He is the One who can deal with it!

HERE AM I, LORD ... SEND SOMEBODY ELSE

SMALL ENOUGH TO DIGEST

The children of Israel had brought a month's supply of food with them: enough to see them into Canaan, "a land flowing with milk and honey" (Exodus 3:8). But now, they found themselves wandering around in circles, taking detours and getting more and more frightened as they watched their precious supply disappear. Two characteristics of a wilderness Christian or a dry disciple are hunger and anger—hunger for bread and anger at God.

After Moses took the Israelites' needs to the Lord, the Lord told Moses He would give them bread from heaven. When they got up the next day, they found a white, frostlike substance on the ground. They ran about asking each other, "What is it?" (The word *manna* literally means "what is it?") After they had collected the manna, they baked it and ate it, finding it sweet to the taste like "wafers made with honey" (Exodus 16:31). This was the food from heaven that fed the children of Israel for their entire forty years of wilderness wanderings. God always has bread for His people!

LIVING BY BREAD ALONE

The story of the miraculous supply of manna is a reminder of many things. First, it reminds us of the grace of God. Then it reminds us of the provision of God. Then it reminds us of the written Word of God.

Jesus said, "Man shall not live on bread alone, but on every word that comes from the mouth of God" (Matthew 4:4). We may try to live by any other means, but it won't be long before we get ravenous for real food!

Maybe we will join a church, knowing somehow our inner hunger pangs have to do with sermons and Bible studies and things like that. We may even try to take notes, but somehow we can't seem to gather enough to satisfy our spiritual hunger. That is because God wants us to gather our own manna from the Bible.

Do we have a right to expect our leaders to produce bread for us at the drop of a hat? Maybe some of you reckon that that's what you are paying the preachers for! After all, they are there to break the Word of God in small enough pieces to nourish us, aren't they? What are they doing with all that free time during the week? But we must remember that however hard they work, our leaders can provide only a certain amount of spiritual nourishment. We are totally dependent on God to supply our daily bread for us. According to the apostle Paul, in Ephesians 4:11–12, the pastor-teacher and other leaders are there to teach and train us to collect our own food. How good is God to allow us a part! So when the Israelites began doing what they did best and started to complain, instead of telling them to quit griping, the God of grace promised His antsy children bread. "I will rain down bread from heaven for you," he told Moses to tell them (Exodus 16:4).

Jesus said, "I am the bread of life" (John 6:35). God rained Jesus on us from heaven one day, and He still expects us to draw our spiritual lives from Him. He is the living Word who spoke to us through His life and actions. Those who understand this wrote about Him, and their words are recorded in the Bible. If we will only read it, those words will help us get to know the very One who is our very food and will teach us how to feed on Him! God patiently worked with the disgruntled multitude. He instructed Moses to instruct them! He gave the Israelites all the information they needed to survive. God wants us to do the same today.

Have you learned how to collect your own manna, or is the Bible still a complete mystery to you? Are you frightened of it? Is it still a big, dark house that you are reluctant to enter? Do you still take a trip to a church once or twice a month and then grumble about the pastor's sermon? By all means go to church, but why don't you buy a Bible, or if you have one, get it down from the top shelf, dust it off, and begin to cook yourself a good meal?

DAY BY DAY BY DAY

First ask yourself, when do I collect the manna of God? The illustration in Exodus 16 gives us some principles for doing that. The people were directed by God through Moses to collect the manna daily. Every day a little manna. They were not to keep it overnight but to get in the habit of collecting it on a daily basis "everyone . . . as much as he needed" (v. 18). And they were not allowed to collect it on the Sabbath at all. In fact, the Sabbath was the only day they were not to collect it! Just imagine if your pastor announced it was against God's law to conduct Bible study on Sunday, but that you had to conduct it daily for yourself, saving up enough for the weekend to share with others. I almost wish pastors would try that sometime and see what would happen.

Some of you may say, "I've been wandering around for years

being bitter at my pastor for not feeding me. I'm so hungry, and I have a terrible case of spiritual malnutrition. I've known somehow I should put all that energy I use complaining into collecting manna, but I just don't know when or how to start!" It may well be you have a valid complaint. Perhaps no one has taken you aside and explained the rudimentary methodology needed to take care of yourself spiritually. Well, "the best way to begin is to begin!" Let me help you.

I suggest you start in the New Testament. Maybe you could read some of Paul's advice to new Christians from the Epistles. Or begin by collecting information about Jesus, the Bread of Life, from one of the Gospels. Read a chapter each day and simply make a list of your findings. At the end you will know Him a little better than when you began.

If you don't want to start in the New Testament, that's all right too. "All Scripture is God-breathed and is useful for teaching, rebuking, correcting and training in righteousness, so that the servant of God may be thoroughly equipped for every good work" (2 Timothy 3:16–17). It's all inspired and inspirational.

Ask yourself questions as you collect a little bit of manna by reading the Scriptures each day. Questions such as, Who is writing this? Who are the characters involved, and where is this happening? What are they doing, and why? What is the reaction of the crowd? Or if you are in an instructional passage of Scripture ask, What does this say? What must it have meant to the people in that day and age? What does it tell me to do today? What does it say to my family, my society, my country, or my world? Ask your pastor or Bible study leader how to collect the manna of the Word of God. If he or she can't tell you, go and find someone who can!

If I was short of physical bread for my temporal body, I know I would leave no stone unturned until I found someone who could tell me how to get some, especially if I had a family to feed. How much more should we be concerned with food for our eternal souls?

EARLY IN THE MORNING

If possible, collect your manna early in the morning. This is exactly what the children of Israel were told to do. I remember learning a simple song when I first began to gather manna in the morning.

> *In the morning first of all,*
> *Savior, let me hear thy call.*
> *Make me ready to obey*
> *Thy commands throughout the day.*

We can apply the idea of collecting manna early in two ways. First, we can apply it to our children, or to ourselves, if we are young in years. The writer of Ecclesiastes stated that if we can establish a habit of collecting manna in the days of our youth, then we can develop a habit that will find us collecting it when we are old. In other words, it's a good idea to remember God while you can remember Him!

If you have children, find some creative Bible readings for them. It was the parents' job to collect the manna for the family members who were too young or old to do it for themselves. Children's questions must be answered. Your little one who wants to know who God is and what He is like has only one person to ask, and that's you. Do you know the answers? Deuteronomy 6:6–7 states, "These commandments that I [God] give you today are to be on your hearts. Impress them on your children. Talk about them when you sit at home and when you walk along the road, when you lie down and when you get up."

The children of Israel were also told to eat the manna while it was fresh. It would not keep for another day, except on the Sabbath. It would go stale, breed worms, and stink! Some Christians are trying to live on manna they collected thirty years ago. It's so stale it has even become obnoxious, just as God said His desert manna would, if it was not absorbed and put to use (Exodus 16:20).

"Oh," some of you may say, "I tried that Bible reading thing, but it went off on me and I went off of it!" Surely it did, because the earthly manna grows stale if not collected new every morning. In the same way the manna you collect is intended to be put to immediate use and turned into life-giving energy at once. This can happen only when it is thoroughly digested.

CHEW IT OVER

To read the Scriptures and to digest the Scriptures are two totally different things—just as seeing and perceiving are different, or hearing and really listening. God told Joshua to "meditate" on His Word (Joshua 1:8). Remember, the word *meditate* means to think a matter through, to chew over, rather like a cow chews the cud so that its body can assimilate it. It's not going to benefit us one bit to simply read our little passage as if it is a lucky charm to keep the evil spirits away. We must mix God's Word with faith, think it through thoroughly, and swallow it. We need to absorb it into our very hearts and minds, and then act on it. Then we will find the strength to be obedient to God's demands.

Collecting manna early can be like a new Christian learning to study the Bible as soon as he or she becomes a believer. You don't have to get a theology degree to go outside your own front door and collect manna. In other words, you can learn to collect your spiritual food for yourself as early as you like in your Christian experience. The apostle Peter wrote, "Like newborn babies, crave pure spiritual milk, so that by it you may grow up in your salvation, now that you have tasted that the Lord is good" (1 Peter 2:2–3).

You will find there is milk and meat in the Bible. The Scriptures contain every diet necessary, from baby food to a full menu for adult appetites. A babe can learn quickly to feed himself. And children don't wait till they are grown to use a knife and fork!

The first day after I became a Christian, Jenny, who had led me to the Lord and given me a Bible, opened it to Luke 5 and said, "Read that and then we'll talk about it." I did, and we did talk about it! It was wonderful. She walked out into a brand-new day with me, showed me where the manna was, and collected it with me. Then we sat down and had a meal together. You can do that for someone else. It could change that person's life.

Collecting manna early can also speak to us of getting ourselves out of bed at the beginning of God's new gift of another day, or as Exodus says, before the sun is hot (16:21). The Lord Jesus had a habit of rising very early in the morning to meet with His Father. He met with God "before daybreak," the Bible says (Mark 1:35 NLT).

Have you ever collected heavenly manna before daybreak? I can really recommend it! Do it before the heat of the day. The cool of the day and the manna of God will prepare you and give you strength to face the monotonous sand dunes that span your horizon or the enemies who lurk around the next corner of your journey of life waiting to bring you down.

GOD ALWAYS HAS BREAD FOR HIS PEOPLE

I have noticed that God always has bread for His people. "Give us food!" the children of Israel demanded. "Go and get it yourselves!" Moses and Aaron retorted. "Gather it according to your eating."[1] There is enough manna to satisfy the most ravenous wilderness Christian. He has promised, as our Shepherd, to lead us into green pastures and teach us to lie down there.

The way a shepherd teaches a sheep to lie down is quite simple, for the sheep is an animal that lies down only when its stomach is full. This shows it is satisfied. Once the sheep is full, it can rest beside the still waters. It does not run around bleating and complaining about its shepherd. The shepherd's responsibility is to lead the flock into green pastures and say, "Go to it!" The sheep's responsibility is to do just that. I believe the antidote for a critical attitude is manna in the morning. Show me a complaining Christian, and I'll show you one who is not collecting his daily food and digesting it, and is therefore unsatisfied. Jesus instructed His followers to pray, "Give us today our daily bread" (Matthew 6:11). He will give it—we should eat it!

I mentioned earlier in this chapter that the Israelites were instructed not to gather any manna on the Sabbath, for there would be none to gather. God did not want them to have to do that on their rest day. So they had to store up enough for their day of rest. When the Sabbath came, they could simply share their stored manna with each other and enjoy it together. It was one day of the week when the bread was to be provided and preserved for the whole family. The manna was to be in the tent, not in the field!

I am quite sure from my own experience that if I faithfully collect and eat my daily manna, when Sunday comes, that which I do not collect for myself, but is provided by my pastor or spiritual leader, is all the more enjoyable. I approach worship with a totally new attitude. I enter my church fellowship with excited anticipation. What the preacher says makes sense. I listen intently. (I always listen with a pencil in my hand. Try it!) This way none of the manna falls to the ground and is wasted. Perhaps I have been grazing the same patch of ground the preacher has been working on. My hunger or appetite is there, of course, for daily hunger requires daily bread, but now, just for once, it is someone else's responsibility to feed me. It is the Lord's Sabbath. I rest from my own labor of collecting my own spiritual food, and I absorb the food served for me in my local church.

MAKE SURE YOU GET A BALANCED DIET

Each of us needs to belong to a fellowship of believers. Insights shared from other people are vital to give us balance and help. Find a place where the manna is believed and broken well from the pulpit. Make sure your pastor and teachers believe that the Word of God "is the bread which the LORD hath given you to eat" (Exodus 16:15 KJV) and are faithfully preaching it. Don't absorb strange food that isn't the inspired, infallible Word of God. Don't look for a change of diet, some modern new recipe that purports to have superseded God's truth as set forward in the Old and New Testaments. Find an evangelical, Bible-believing "tent," and be there on the Sabbath to share and eat together. This is the Lord's command.

There was a small group of Israelites who didn't think all this was at all necessary. "Some of the people went out on the seventh day to gather it, but they found none" (v. 27). They were arrogant and disobedient, and God was rightly frustrated with them.

In my experience, I have met such people, and I must confess they irritate me too. There is a danger of new Christians who, having been encouraged to gather manna for themselves, decide they don't need any Christian fellowship on the Sabbath. They become proud and independent. We are told not to do that! "Let us not neglect our meeting together, as some people do, but encourage one another" (Hebrews 10:24–25 NLT).

God has commanded every man to go to "the tent of meeting" for fellowship on God's day, and those who insist on staying away and doing without it will soon become impoverished. Fellowship and food are in the tents; that's where God has ordained them to be, and that is where we are to be to receive and to enjoy them.

I have met groups of young Christians who feel they don't need to identify with a body of believers. They meet and study the Bible or watch videos in isolation. But the structure of the authority of the church, as laid down in the Epistles, is missing. To those who go out on their own on the Sabbath, God would say, as He did to the children of Israel, "How long will you refuse to keep my commands and my instructions?" (Exodus 16:28). We all need to be in God's house on the Sabbath, listening to our undershepherds and sharing the manna we have collected and laid up with others, instead of deciding that "those immature people and these shallow shepherds can't teach us anything!"

In summary, learn early to collect your daily manna. Our God-appointed shepherds should instruct us carefully how to do this as we gather in our tents once a week to share together. This is a commandment of the Lord. We are to stop complaining against Moses and Aaron, for our complaints are not against man but are really against God, who hears our mumblings and is deeply disappointed with us! In Numbers 14:27, the Lord inquires about the Israelites' complaining: "How long shall I bear with this evil congregation who are grumbling against Me?" (NASB). How long indeed!

There is no way we can enter into that land of promised victory in our Christian experience if we do not nourish ourselves from the living Word of God. God has said so, and we will simply spend years wandering around and around in ever-decreasing evangelical circles till we die in our desert—still grumbling and still hungry! Get up before daybreak and collect your daily manna in the morning so you can obey His commands. Be in your tent faithfully on the Sabbath, sharing with others and resting. Don't put aside discernment, but respect your human and fallible guides, knowing a divine and infallible God has invested them with His authority. This way you will be well on your way to Canaan.

It's time to discover, discuss, and then apply the discoveries you have made. If you are using this for your own study time, record your findings in a notebook.

Summary

In a sentence or two, summarize what this chapter is about.

Discovery

Read Exodus 16. What else do you see that we didn't cover in the chapter?

Discussion or Journal

1. Have you ever looked back or gone back? Why?
2. Share some nourishing manna you discovered this week.
3. Share among your group the helpful ideas you each use in a devotional time.

Decision

1. What in this chapter most applies to you? What do you need to do about it?
2. Think about your habits. Do you need to repent about grumbling?
3. Share your decision and pray about it with a partner.

Devotion

Here is a practical plan for one week of manna for your spiritual needs.

- *Monday.* Read Paul's advice to new Christians in Philippians 4:1–9. Underline all the commands you find in this passage. Pray to God, asking for help in keeping them.
- *Tuesday.* Read John 4:1–42 and write down all the things Jesus did in this incident that we need to do for others as we witness to them. Pray that God will show you one individual you can talk to about Him.
- *Wednesday.* Read Luke 8:22–25. Ask yourself these questions: Who is writing this? Who is it about? What is happening? Why? When? What does this show me of Jesus? What does it show me about myself?
- *Thursday.* Read Romans 8. Underline all the promises. Pray that God will help your unbelief. Pray that others who need these promises will appropriate them.
- *Friday.* Read 1 Corinthians 15:58. Write down ten things this verse tells you. Search diligently, and you will find them! Follow the same procedure for 2 Timothy 2:15 and James 1:12.
- *Saturday.* Read James 1:25 and memorize it. Why? Read Psalm 119:9–11. That's why!
- *Sunday.* Read the entire book of Ephesians, without stopping. Pray about the verses that were most meaningful to you.

A Personal Spiritual Workout

1. Mark in your calendar a time each day this coming week when you will collect your manna.
2. Make a list of hindrances to your quiet time. Pray about them.

SEVEN

ROCK OF AGES

Our home in Wisconsin is located in a beautiful country district, and for this reason we are dependent on a well for water. One day, like the woman at the well, I found myself seeking. Our well was dry, and I had to telephone the local well diggers. They told me how much per foot it would cost to drill deep enough to find water, but they couldn't tell me how deep that would be because they didn't know. They could say only that it would be a costly enterprise. It was. But not nearly as costly an enterprise as finding spiritual water for a dying spirit and soul! That enterprise cost the Son of God His life on the cross.

The analogy of the Spirit of God as the water of life abounds in Scripture. The lessons to this end that the children of Israel were about to learn were surely graphic and unforgettable ones. Man can survive without food for quite a while, but to live without water is quite another thing. When you live in a desert, you are continually reminded that you need a drink. God's people required a source of water to survive in their wilderness, and we too need a source of water to survive in the desert of the world in which we live. Our dry spirits cry out continually for refreshment (Exodus 17:1–7).

Listen to the multitude crying out for water. "They quarreled with Moses and said, 'Give us water to drink.' Moses replied, 'Why do you quarrel with me? Why do you put the LORD to the test?' But the people were thirsty for water there, and they grumbled against Moses. They said, 'Why did you bring us up out of Egypt to make us and our children and livestock die of thirst?' Then Moses cried out to the LORD, "What am I to do with these people? They are almost ready to stone me'" (vv. 2–4).

God told Moses that He would stand before him on this special rock in Mount Horeb and that Moses was to strike the rock with his rod. Moses' rod represented God's authority, while the rock depicted Jesus Christ, who was to be struck by the rod of God's wrath on the cross. When the rock was smitten, the water was released. The miracle of the gushing water is a beautiful picture of the One who was to be the source of Israel's survival—the blessed Holy Spirit.

We need be in no doubt as to the analogy of Christ and the rock because the apostle Paul lays it out for us in 1 Corinthians 10:3–4. Speaking of Israel's wanderings in the desert and using them to teach lessons from their history, Paul says, "They all ate the same spiritual food and drank the same spiritual drink; for they drank from the spiritual rock that accompanied them, and that rock was Christ."

One of the first hymns I sang as a new believer was "Rock of Ages." I remember standing in a beautiful Anglican church in Cambridge, singing those words with tears running down my cheeks. I had been living in such a desperate desert of self-gratification. Nothing satisfied me; nothing filled me up; nothing quenched my inner craving for peace. Like the woman who met Jesus at the well, I was lowering my bucket in "the well of my wantings" and coming up dry.

God wants us to have that continual craving for Him met and satisfied. He is the source of our satisfaction, but we must always remember what a costly enterprise it was for God to "dig deeper," to reach that rich water vein of the life of the Son of God so we could drink freely of the Spirit. It wasn't until the Roman soldiers nailed the Son of God to the cross that He finished the work of supplying our redemption.

> *Rock of Ages, cleft for me,*
> *Let me hide myself in Thee;*
> *Let the water and the blood,*
> *From Thy riven side that flowed,*
> *Be of sin the double cure,*
> *Cleanse me from its guilt and power.*

Standing in that ancient pew in that ancient church, I sobbed my way through my response:

> *Nothing in my hand I bring,*
> *Simply to Thy cross I cling;*
> *Naked, come to Thee for dress;*
> *Helpless, come to Thee for grace;*
> *Foul, I to the fountain fly,*
> *Wash me, Savior, or I die![1]*

Ever since that experience, the picture of the smitten rock has brought me to tears. Thousands of years ago God was drawing pictures in the sand for Israel, and they learned another lesson. Do you get the picture too? Sinful man must come to the smitten Rock and in desperate need receive the Spirit, the Water of Eternal Life. That is the beginning.

DON'T SAY, "I'M THE ONLY ONE"; SAY, "I'M THE FIRST ONE"

But this is only the beginning! From that point on, we need to daily gather our manna and drink of the Spirit. What does that mean? It means that as we daily speak to the risen Rock about our thirst, the Spirit will continue to supply us. Perhaps we are thirsty for *companionship*. Maybe you are the only Christian in your family, and you feel so alone. As my friend once encouraged me, don't say, "I'm the only one." Start saying, "I'm the first one." As you wait for your loved ones to put their trust in Jesus, begin to trust the Rock to supply your need of companionship through the Spirit. His name is "the Comforter," and He will be the One called alongside to help, just as Jesus promised in John 14:26. You may be alone, but you need never be lonely.

Perhaps you are thirsty for *excitement* or change in your schedule. Your life seems so dull, drab, and monotonous. You have really been able to identify with all these people wandering around in circles and getting nowhere for forty years. Except in your case, it feels like eighty years! Speak to the Rock, and the Spirit will supply your need.

In Genesis 1:2, the writer stated there was once a situation without form. It was void. Just a deep hole. Nothingness. You couldn't even see anything, because darkness was on the face of the deep. Is that a little like a description of your life—even though God is your Father and Christ is your Savior? Well, look what is stated in the verse: The Spirit of God moved on the face of that whole situation. God began to speak, and the Spirit supplied His intentions. New light, new life, and new love all came to being in that monotonous landscape. Every day something new happened that had never happened before. That can be your experience too. God not only brings order out of chaos, but He can give you the "Genesis week" of your life!

Speak to the Rock about your need, and God will do something He has never done before for anyone else, and He will do it every day. He may not transport you from your environment, but He will touch your situation with His creative genius. Being the originator of all creativity, God won't get stuck for a new idea to brighten up your dull landscape. He doesn't copy something He has done for someone else either. Each creative act is unique because you are unique. Ask God for a genesis in your life, and you'll see it will be very, very good. He will turn the monotonous into the momentous. Pray, "Oh Lord, create a Genesis week in my life!"

> Order out of chaos,
> Light in darkest things,
> Revive my fainting spirit, Lord,
> Until my heart takes wings.
> Till Right rights all the wrongnesses,
> Till heaven *is* one day.
> Till Grace binds up my deepest wounds,

And peace has come to stay.
Spinning out of all control,
I need Your steadying hand
To slow me down enough to see
The order You have planned.
God make a new creation now,
And hover o'er my soul.
Oh, Lord of sun and moon and stars,
Please come and make me whole.
Bring order out of chaos,
Bring peace within the pain.
Speak Jesus in my life, dear Lord,
And bid me live again.

Perhaps you are thirsty for order in your chaotic life. Speak to the Rock!

Maybe you are thirsty for appreciation. No one seems to really understand how hard you work, and you never seem to receive a word of thanks. Perhaps you are a stepparent trying your level best to invest in the children you have inherited. Nobody seems to care; nobody notices. Speak to the Rock. He notices and appreciates all your efforts.

Maybe no one even seems to notice the effort it takes to do that insignificant duty in church. Nobody seems to care if you turn up or not at the group meeting. They never ask you to help, or if they do, they forget to notice it or to repay you. You're so thirsty for someone to need you; you need so much to be needed!

Speak to the Rock; He needs you. He's never given life to an unimportant person. Each of you is significant. Your Savior notices, and He watches you work. He always says thank you, for in 1 Corinthians 13:5, Paul wrote, "Love has good manners" (PHILLIPS; see also Hebrews 6:10). God asks you to do something very special for Him: He asks you to be His "ambassador" down here, representing the King of kings and Lord of lords (2 Corinthians 5:20). Yes, little you! God trusts you with messages to the people you live among, and He trusts you to represent Him faithfully. How privileged can you be? If you aim to please God instead of trying to please the church, then His "well done" will be the only appreciation you will be looking for.

Perhaps you are thirsty for the power to be different. You crave the power to stop doing some of the things you wish you could stop doing and to start doing things you know you should. Speak to the Rock. The Spirit will make the power you need operative in your life.

HERE COMES AMALEK

Maybe you want to ask, "What does it mean to 'speak to the Rock'?" Well, I'm really talking about prayer: the speaking part of our relationship with the Source of our spiritual survival. Prayer releases the power we need to be Christlike. When you are battling with your own personal thirst, you need to speak in prayer to the Rock. The very next part of our text, Exodus 17:8–16, illustrates this beautifully.

As soon as Israel had been instructed about the source of their help, Amalek came and fought with them. It's just as if God teaches us a lesson and then takes us on a field trip to test it out. It's like learning driving theory in the classroom and then being told it's time to get into the car! Theory and practice must go together. We need opportunities to work out what God is working in (Philippians 2:13).

Amalek was a tribe of people opposed to God. They were strong and didn't like God's people; in fact, they were the Israelites' avowed enemy. Amalek can be to us a picture of the "flesh," or self. The Bible tells us God vowed He would have war with Amalek throughout all generations (Exodus 17:16). Selfishness must have less and less part in our lives once we are rescued from being self-centered and become God-centered.

At the start of World War II, England declared war on Germany after the German invasion of Poland. Soon, other nations acknowledged that war had been declared and joined in. They became England's allies. Once we recognize God has declared war on selfishness, it behooves us to join in. We need to become allied with God in His declaration of war against the Enemy. This means we will meet Amalek on the battlefield of our own hearts. God never promised His people a playground! Rather, He promised us a battleground.

One of the things you will discover as a new Christian is that the self does not die the moment you receive Christ. He may be momentarily stunned, but he does not die. It is often a complete surprise to new Christians to have the first rosy hue of their newborn experience die away and be faced with an enemy like Amalek. These new Christians just don't expect such raw self-centeredness in their new life, and when Amalek confronts them, his sudden appearance can result in overwhelming defeat. The children of Israel were well into their new experience, and then Amalek came and fought with them. I believe he took them by surprise. Until the day we die, you and I will be confronted by Amalek. To help you recognize him, here is a word portrait of your enemy self—or "the flesh"—taken from Ruth Paxson's classic book, *Life on the Highest Plane*:

Self-will—"We have turned every one to his own way." The flesh wants its own way and is determined to have it even if it defies and disobeys God and overrides others. "I will" is the alphabet out of which self fashions its language of life.

Self-centeredness—"the old man" feeds upon himself. He is the beginning and the end. Life presents little that interests or affects him except as it relates to himself. He is the center of the world in which he lives and moves and he always looks out for number one.

Self-assertion—"the old man" believes that everyone is as interested in him and as fascinated by him as he himself is, so he protrudes and projects himself into the sight, hearing and notice of others continually. He monopolizes conversation and the theme is always "I," "my" and "mine." He walks with a swagger and expects the world to stop work and look at him. And he never dreams how offensive his self-importance is to others.

Self-depreciation—"the old man" is very versatile and sometimes it suits his purpose better to clothe his pride in a false humility. He curls up in his self-depreciation and shirks a lot of hard work which other people have to do. He magnifies his littleness and feebleness to his own advantage, yet with strange inconsistency he resents others taking seriously his professed estimate of himself and treating him accordingly.

Self-conceit—"the old man" lives so much in himself that he does not know how big the world is in which he lives and how many other really intelligent people there are in it, so he has little regard for the opinions of others, especially if contrary to his own. He looks with proud and supercilious pity upon those less favored and gifted than himself.

Self-love—"the old man" loves himself supremely, one might say almost exclusively. He loves God not at all and his human love for others is tainted more or less with selfishness, jealousy, envy or impurity. . . .

Self-sufficiency—the self-confidence of "the old man" fosters an egotistical, smug self-satisfaction, which leaves him stagnant. He has neither desire nor sense of need for anything beyond what he already possesses.

Self-consciousness—"the old man" never forgets himself: wherever he goes he casts a shadow of himself before. He is constantly occupied with photographing himself and developing the plates. He is chained to himself and as he walks one hears the clank of the chains. He is often morbidly self-introspective.

Self-exaltation—"the old man" is absorbed in his own excellencies: he overestimates himself and his abilities: he thirsts for admiration and praise and he thrives on flattery. He secretly worships at the shrine "self," and he wishes others to do so publicly.

Self-righteousness—"the old man" loves to dress himself in the garments of morality, benevolence and public-spiritedness. He even patronizes the church and often assists in drives for raising money for philanthropic and religious purposes, heading the list of donors with a handsome gift. He keeps a double entry account book—both with the church and with the world and expects a reward both on earth and in heaven.

Self-glorying—perhaps "the old man" resents this plain delineation of himself as he really is and thinks the condemnation too sweeping. Immediately he begins to enumerate his good qualities, his amiableness, geniality, tolerance, self-control, sacrificial spirit and other virtues. In doing so, he takes all the credit to himself for what he is, exhibiting ill-concealed pride and vanity.[2]

Did you recognize your self in this description of "the old man"? I did!

JUST SAY NO

To know and recognize your enemy is half the battle. Joshua took his fighting forces and engaged the enemy in a terrible fight. Some people say that God will fight for you; all you do is let Him. Don't do anything! Well, I don't buy that. The Scriptures say you have a part to play. You have to do one thing. You have to resist the Devil by saying no to selfish acts and selfish thoughts. "Resist the devil, and he will flee from you" (James 4:7). That's an order, and it involves work. The word *resist* means to actively oppose. It means to "just say no."

Are you trying to tell me Joshua didn't put out any effort that memorable day? Read the story in Exodus 17, and then tell me he didn't do anything. Joshua was fighting, all right, but his battle in the valley was balanced by the battle on the mountaintop where Moses, Aaron, and Hur were keeping watch over the events in the valley below.

Praying on the mountaintop has incredible power for the people in the valley! There was a missionary in the last century who went out from England to Asia. His home church split and then dissipated. It was the only support he was receiving. The situation left him stranded in Asia without support. The biggest dilemma he faced, however, was not lack of funds as he got a job and supported himself, but lack of prayer! He wrote home to a friend, "I am unprayed for. I feel it. I feel like a deep-sea diver with no oxygen, or like a fireman on a burning building with an empty hose." That's what it's like when you are unprayed for! Joshua didn't feel like that because he was prayed for by three men on a hill, holding on to the authority of God over the situation on his behalf. These three men positioned themselves to watch over Joshua until he prevailed.

What are you trying to "just say no" to? Is it a habit to do with drinking or drugs? Is it a temper that gets you into constant trouble? Is someone maligning your character or suing your husband or ruining your kids? What's the battle all about? Well, recruit some prayer warriors and just say no to your difficult circumstances as your prayer partners support you in your fight with Amalek.

The symbol of the authority of the God of Israel was in Moses' hand—"the rod of God" (Exodus 17:9 KJV). As Moses held this rod above the whole situation, he spoke to the Lord about Joshua and his battle. Joshua was fighting, but the God of Israel fought for him. Over and over again in the Old Testament narrative, we read these words: "And God fought for Israel." But whenever you read this, you will see that Israel was fighting too.

The battle was won before the Israelites began fighting, because they knew they had the Lord God of hosts on their side. Yet the battle still had to be fought. You have to meet the Enemy and engage in the struggle. You have to stand your ground and refuse to move. There is no victory without a battle. But with the Lord God of Israel on your side, you can know that victory is secured. You can know, even as you see the Enemy approaching, that he is beaten. God is stronger than Amalek. You're not, but God will strengthen you as you fight, until you are! Remember that the apostle John wrote, "The one who is in you is greater than the one who is in the world" (1 John 4:4).

THE BATTLE IS WON
BEFORE IT BEGINS

You have to believe the rod of God is held over you. God is in control. The authority of His Word says, "Sin shall no longer be your master" (Romans 6:14). Self need not win the battle. God promises that you can win whatever battle you are fighting, but God also commands you to do your part. We have to appropriate the forces available. Our part is to say no to selfishness and to seek a Moses, an Aaron, and a Hur to sit on the mountain and pray for us.

Look at this prayer team! When Moses' arms got weary holding the authority of God over the situation, Aaron and Hur took a stone and Moses sat on it. Then they each took a place beside Moses and held up his weary arms till the battle was won! During our children's teenage years, I gathered some of their friends' parents together at our house, and we kept watch over the battle in the valley together. We held each other's hands up when they felt weary until those scary years were over and God had won the battle for their minds and hearts and lives. Now I have started all over again as a grandmother praying for thirteen grandchildren! All of us can find an Aaron or a Hur to stand against the Devil on others' behalf and resist him in prayer.

I have also experienced winning a battle over self-will as my prayer partners have engaged in fervent prayer on my behalf, and I have sensed a weakening when they become weary. That's why having two or three prayer partners is a good idea. When one gets tired, the other two hold up his or her hands.

Matthew 18:18–20 records Christ's exhortation to gather together with two or three believers to pray. Joshua knew what it was to watch from the mountain for others, but he also knew he needed prayer help when it was his turn to fight. So when Amalek comes, you are going to need reminding of God's authority over sin, selfishness, and Satan. God's Word is His bond, and He promised the battle will be won, but you will need help.

You can also help others who are fighting Amalek. There is no greater privilege than holding up one's hands to heaven and claiming God's mastery for a Joshua in the valley. Ask God to remind the strugglers in the valley of His sovereignty and the potential victory that can be claimed. The authority of His Word should be used to hold back Satan's forces from the scene. However young a Christian you may be, you are called to this ministry of prayer.

God didn't tell Israel to humor Amalek, pamper him, ignore him, or make an alliance or truce with him. There was to be no compromise. He was to be put away. Does that mean we can kill selfishness? No! We will never be totally free until the day of our funeral. In fact, as far as those of us who die are concerned, it won't be our funeral at all—it will be the death of our old natures and our birth into heaven. One day the "old man" will be put away just as Satan will be. Until that time, God promises we can live as if our old self is dead already. We can pay no attention to his needs. We can ignore his demands.

We can drive him out of our territory. But how? One way is to begin to starve him out.

WHICH NATURE ARE YOU FEEDING?

I heard an illustration once of a bird called the cuckoo. The cuckoo always lays its eggs in another bird's nest. When Mrs. Birdie, the nest's owner, comes along, she doesn't bother counting the eggs. She has to work her feathers to the bone hatching this huge monstrosity of an egg, this foreign nature she finds in her nest. When hatched, the baby cuckoo begins to steal the worms Mrs. Birdie finds, and it soon grows big enough to tip the starving chicks out. Thereafter the cuckoo reigns supreme.

The two natures in that one nest show our condition. In our lives, we have selfishness and Jesus, by His Spirit, living within. The nature that prospers and grows, eventually gaining dominion, depends on us to feed it. So the question is, which nature are you feeding? That nature will dominate your life, your thinking, and your actions.

If Amalek had stayed put in his walled city, Joshua could have tried starving him out. That's one method of dealing with him, and you could try it too. Make sure you are feeding God's nature by feeding on and obeying the Word of God. Be careful of what you read and watch on television. Remember: Garbage in, garbage out!

As it happened, Amalek attacked Israel, and Israel had to stand firm and resist, then counterattack with prayer to drive him off. Likewise, you can always stand firm and say no. Oh yes, you can. God says so. However weak it sounds, even a whispered no will be sufficient to turn the Devil away. You can say no just as easily as you can say yes. You have to say no without feeling no sometimes! Whatever you do, don't trust your feelings in a battle; do what you are told, and not what you feel. Actively oppose Amalek by saying no to self and yes to God, and then act as if you mean it. The feelings will follow.

So speak to the Rock about your own needs: the needs for companionship, excitement, appreciation, and the power to be different. Speak also to the Rock about your brothers' and sisters' needs in the valley in the heat of the battle. Learn to pray on their behalf, claiming God's authority over hostile situations. But learn to fight as well. Ask God to help you to hate what He hates—Amalek, the picture of selfishness—and determine either to starve him out or to resist him. Remember above all, "the battle is the LORD's" (1 Samuel 17:47).

It's time to discover, discuss, and then apply the discoveries you have made. If you are using this for your own study time, record your findings in a notebook.

Summary

In a sentence or two, summarize what this chapter is about.

Discovery

Read the following Scriptures and answer the questions about the Rock.

1. *The Old Testament*
   a. In Deuteronomy 32:4, the Rock is identified for us. Who is He?
   b. In Deuteronomy 32:28–30 what is said about Israel's enemies, concerning their source of support?
   c. In 2 Samuel 23:3, David makes a statement concerning the Rock. What is it?

2. *The New Testament*
   a. Here we see the Rock represents Christ as well. Read 1 Corinthians 10:4 to see the Rock identified.
   b. What are we told in Ephesians 2:20?
   c. What does Romans 9:32–35 add to our information?
   d. Read Daniel 2:34 and note an Old Testament fact that will become a future reality. See also Matthew 21:44.

3. *The Smitten Rock.* In Matthew 26:31, Christ quotes from Zechariah 13:7, "I will strike the shepherd." The smitten or stricken Rock produces the flow of the Spirit, to sustain and satisfy God's people. The water of life is necessary for Canaan living. Read John 4:1–14. Jesus claimed his ability to impart living water to satisfy the soul. Read John 7:37–39 and identify the living water.

Discussion or Journal

1. The Holy Spirit is holy. Therefore, He cannot abide with selfishness. In fact, He cannot be satis-

fied unless war is declared on Amalek—a picture
of our selfish nature.

   a. Where did Amalek come from (Genesis 36:12),
     and what was his nature?

   b. Read Deuteronomy 25:17–19, and answer these
     questions:

     (1) How does Amalek attack us?

     (2) When does Amalek attack us?

     (3) What is God's command to Israel, and us?

2. Discuss God's intentions for Amalek, as described in Exodus 17:16. An example of a Christian
who has not declared war on Amalek and is al-
lowing himself to be overcome in battle is found
in James 4:4–7.

Decision

1. Apply this teaching about Amalek to your own
life.

2. Whom will you invite to pray for you as you
battle Amalek?

3. When will you invite them?

Devotion

1. Pray through the discoveries you have made
while reading this chapter.

2. Spend some time in quietness, thinking about
God's intentions and provisions for you.

A Personal Spiritual Workout

Each day choose a thought or look up a verse in your notes pertaining to the lessons learned, and *meditate* (which means "to chew it over") throughout the day. Pray about it each night.

EIGHT

THE SCHOOLMASTER

Ecclesiastes says that God has "set eternity in the human heart" (3:11). Human beings are religious at heart, and religion itself is as universal as man. So humans are spiritual entities and cannot help believing in something outside their frame of reference. That's what makes them different from the animals. They possess an innate sense, as C. S. Lewis said in *Mere Christianity*, that they are "made for another world."[1] The animals do not kneel to pray—or ours don't anyway! But there is an inside something built into man's makeup that tells him, as the old spiritual song goes,

> *This world is not my home;*
> *I'm just a' passing through.*

The seeking heart of humanity cries out, "There is Someone, somewhere in the universe outside of myself whom I need to know and reach out to."

Wherever you go in the world, you'll discover a belief in another being or beings that demands worship. Traveling as I do, I have seen the most primitive people worshipping their gods. Some think these gods live in trees, rivers, or even stones. Yet I have also watched a well-dressed businessman in downtown Tokyo stop and leave a Coke—a drink offering—at the base of a tree outside a towering tech building before he begins high-powered transactions across the globe! Now you might say, "What about the Communists? They don't believe in a superior being, and they don't worship anything." Oh, but they do; they worship the state.

RELIGION AND THEOLOGY

Religion gives us the concept of God; that's what religion is all about. It says, "Hey there, did you know that God exists?" Theology collects all the ideas about this Being and seeks to order them and give them content. Then it indexes them for us to examine. That's what theology is all about—it is a study of God. Religion gives the idea of God, and theology collects the facts, tidies them up, and records them.

Not all religions have been able to do this. Only in a few highly developed ones do you find systematic tabulations. That's why some religions of the past never lasted. They didn't have any doctrine. The thoughts or words about what God said weren't preserved or passed on to others. They didn't survive because there wasn't anyone to think through the things they were saying about their ideas of God and capture them in some fashion.

Brahmanism, Buddhism, Judaism, Islam, and Christianity

are some of the higher systems of religious thought, and they all have a theology. These are some of the great thought systems of our world. Most of the recorded religions believe in a divine being and in man's relationship to Him, even though they conceive of Him in different ways.

WHICH ONE IS RIGHT?

The problem facing you and me is to determine which one in this array of beliefs is right. Is everybody a little bit right? Or is one religion all right? Not only can this be a puzzle, but it can result in complete confusion for many people. Wherever you go in the world, new thoughts and ideas have added a cacophony of voices to the mix. Yet as you look at these "new" religions, you begin to agree with Solomon: "There is nothing new under the sun" (Ecclesiastes 1:9).

If you go back to the beginning of history, you can read about man's involvement in animism, fetishism, polytheism, henotheism, pantheism, deism, and more. Most of these primitive people worshipped spirits. They didn't worship an object; the object simply represented the spirit who lived within it. For example, in animism, the idol that a man came to worship could have been a tree. The tree would represent the spirit that lived inside it, or the sun would represent the spirit that sent the sun. This innate sense that there was a spirit world seems to have been around as long as man has been around.

These ancient people believed in God as a Spirit, and they made an effort to reach out to Him. Believe it or not, it's possible to recognize some of the elements of these ancient belief systems as they have surfaced in the twenty-first century in the form of New Age religions and the like.

For example, there has been a syncretism in Europe, where Christianity has been declining. I heard about a girl who went into a shop and was looking for a little gold cross to give to her daughter. Whatever they sell, most shops usually have a tray of paraphernalia on the checkout counter, consisting of a mixture of trinkets and symbols to hang around your neck or to carry with you, which among other things people believe will ward off bad luck. The girl asked for a cross, and the young woman serving there willingly obliged and began rummaging through the tray.

"Why, here are two of them," she announced triumphantly, her search rewarded. "But look at that!" she exclaimed. "They're not the same. There's a little man on one of them." This truly happened in "my" England! I cried when I heard this story, because I knew the girl was not being blasphemous; she just didn't know the gospel story of Jesus Christ and His love.

To her the trinkets on the counter represented all the religious options you could choose from. All had equal validity, even the one with the little man on it! She had no idea the "little man" was her Savior. The girl who came to buy the cross told her!

Are we up to the challenge? Are we cognizant of the new beliefs that are swirling around beyond the Christian community where we live and move and have our being? Do we have classes in our churches to study the plethora of belief systems around us, and can we engage someone in a spiritually intelligent conversation and explain the gospel using terms he or she understands? Are we contemporaneously relevant, or do we say "Here am I, Lord . . . send the youth specialist"?

The problem with all these religions, other than Christianity and Judaism, is that they are all man's ideas about God. It is like a man building a tower to heaven to get near enough to see God and figure Him out all by his clever little self.

There was a time in biblical history when men actually *did* build a tower with this very thing in mind at a place called Babel. They wanted to see God up close and personal. *Babel* means confusion, and that is where these people attempting this search in their own strength and prowess ended up. That is where we shall all end up, too, if we dispense with God's help and depend instead on our own IQ, high-tech methods, or speculation.

Christianity claims that God has taken the initiative and revealed Himself to man, so it is not a question of man's speculative philosophy, but of revealed theology. It's as though God has said, "I will tell you what I'm like, I will tell you what I think, I will tell you how I feel, and I will show you what I'll do! I will even come down and become one of you so you can really understand Me. I will speak with a man's voice because I will be a man. I will live in a man's house, I will eat a man's food, and I will meet you face-to-face." Read John 14:8–9, and see that Jesus Christ said essentially these things to Philip.

There is no religion in the world, apart from Christianity, that claims God became man and yet kept His divine nature. The letter to the Philippians tells us that Jesus Christ laid aside His glory—that is, the trappings of His deity—when He visited our tiny globe and was born at Bethlehem. Jesus didn't lay aside His deity itself but He left heaven in order that He might experience the incarnation and, through His plan of redemption, save us.

There is also no other religion in the world that tells of a God-Man's death and resurrection. Paul says, "If Christ has not been raised, our preaching is useless and so is your faith"

(1 Corinthians 15:14). We will never share our faith naturally and easily if we do not have a grasp of biblical truth and passionately believe it!

We have so much help available to us today, not only in teaching, books, videos, and the like, but in the Scriptures. More than anything we need to read the Bible account.

In the Old Testament we can see the dramatic way that God explained His character and will in the story of his giving humankind the Ten Commandments.

CLIMB THE MOUNTAIN

One day God told Moses to climb a mountain and meet Him there face-to-face. We need to climb our mountain like Moses did. We must put out the effort to find out what God is like and what He wants and expects from us. But how do we search out God? And how do we receive His revealed truth?

How did God tell the people who were alive in Old Testament times about His intentions? Among other things, He met them on a famous mountain called Sinai and spoke in an intelligible way to one of them—Moses, by name. We can hear the same voice if we read the account in Exodus. Just open the Bible and follow Moses up the mountain in your imagination.

If I were God, and I had made you and wanted to talk to you, how should I do it? I'd probably use a human sort of voice that you would be familiar with and therefore understand. So it is no problem to me to accept that God spoke with a voice. In Deuteronomy 4:36, the writer stated, "From heaven he made you hear his voice . . . and you heard his words." What did God say? What was the message for the world that He told Moses to write down? Well now, that is quite a story. It involves poor old Moses getting some serious exercise. It wasn't just what God said to him that's so interesting, but where God said what He said (Exodus 19).

First of all, God called Moses up to the top of Mount Sinai. As soon as Moses got up to the top of the mountain, God said, "Now I want you to go down to the bottom of the mountain and tell the people that tomorrow you are going to meet with me." So Moses wound his weary way back down to the bottom of the mountain. He got the people together and said, "Listen to me! Tomorrow is going to be a very special day. You know that cloud that's been leading us all this way? Well, that same visible manifestation of the invisible God is actually going to cover this mountain. I am supposed to go up into the glory cloud and meet with God. Then I'll come back and tell you what He said."[2]

So all the people got cleaned up and ready to meet God. The next day, Moses climbed to the top of the mountain again. God came down, there was fire and a great shaking of the ground, and the people down below were petrified. Moses, I'm quite sure, was quaking too, but he must have had a fantastic sense of exhilaration and anticipation. He was ready to find out what God wanted to say to the human race, when the Lord said, "Moses, I want you to go down there and warn those people not to touch the mountain, because if they do, they are going to die!" Now, as you can well appreciate, Moses was somewhat pooped by now; all those times up and down Sinai weren't like jogging around a desert track! Maybe Moses wanted to suggest he might die in the doing of God's will, but instead he protested weakly, "The people cannot come up Mount Sinai, because you yourself warned us, 'Put limits around the mountain and set it apart as holy'" (v. 23). But the Lord said, "Go down and bring Aaron up with you" (v. 24), and there was nothing for Moses to do but to obey.

Why all the hassle? God was trying to teach Moses and the people how dangerous it is for sinful men and women to approach a holy God, and how important God's words are. They are surely worth the effort of climbing a mountain three times in two days. If the sight of God made a mountain quake, what should we do when we hear God's voice through the Scriptures? How awesome that should be. Do we approach God's Word in the same attitude of fear and reverence that Moses did? I think not!

God's words are the most marvelous and frightening things in this world, yet some of us cannot remember more than two of the Ten Commandments, and most of us wouldn't even walk two blocks to inquire about them, much less exert ourselves like Moses did. Climb the mountain of faith and take the time to get it straight. We need to be sure of what God says, why He says it, to whom He wants to say it, what happens if we accept and obey His laws, and what happens if we don't.

Let me give you a definition of *law* before we continue: A *law* is a rule laid down by an intelligent being for the guidance and instruction of another intelligent being. We are made with the ability to know that God exists and to be able to find out what He wants from us. So if we can exert our intelligence to understand the rules laid down for our guidance by this supernatural intelligent being, then we are going to find a way of living, a philosophy that will guide us into making intelligent, biblical sense out of life.

BIBLE SCHOOL

Remember that just before this event, the children of Israel had come from slavery to freedom. They'd been delivered from hard labor into life. It had been like a birth experience, and now they had a new existence. Some of you are like that. You've come to Christ from one sort of life into another. You have received a brand-new start. It's been like a new birth (and that's what it is, says John 3:3–21), and you have begun to grow, as all babies grow. Then after babies grow into children, it's time to go to school.

That time had come for the children of Israel to go to school. God was about to introduce them to their teacher, whose name was Mr. Law. Do you remember your first teacher? I think most of us do. I remember mine had a big nose! I don't remember anything else about her, but that nose seemed to fill my world for weeks after I started school!

Those of you who have children will recall after that first day of school, asking your child, "What is your teacher like?" That's the thing that has been occupying all of your minds. The child has been wondering, *Will she be welcoming? Will she be cruel? Will she understand if I don't get A's all the time? Will she like me? Will I like her?* What consternation if the child returns home from school and says, "I don't like her and I don't think she likes me! She keeps telling me what to do, and when I try to do it, she scolds me and says I haven't done it right."

Mr. Law was like that. Mr. Law was Israel's teacher (see Galatians 3:23–24). He was a hard schoolmaster. In fact, he was very difficult indeed, and Israel decided they did not like going to school! He seemed to demand perfection all the time. Since that day, man in general has not liked going to school either.

Especially when people find out who is waiting for them in the classroom! So why did God give the Law to the children of Israel in the first place?

THE LAW DIDN'T GET THE PEOPLE OUT OF EGYPT

Notice, the Law was given to a free people. Now this is very important. The Law was not given to them to get them out of Egypt. The Law was given to them *after* they had been saved by the death of the Passover lamb. People are making a big mistake today. They think the Law was given to get them out of Egypt—to save them, so they can go to heaven. They believe if they keep God's rules—Mr. Law's demands—then God will give them a passing grade and welcome them into heaven! But the book of Exodus teaches us that the children of Israel were delivered by the sacrifice of the Passover lamb. There had to be a life given, blood shed. That is the only way we can be delivered from Satan's hand, not by obeying Mr. Law in the school of life. The Law was given to a delivered people and was not the means of escape from Egypt. Faith in applying the blood of the lamb was the only way to escape the judgment of God . . . and don't let us forget it!

Then why the Law? And does it have any relevance to people who don't believe in Jesus? If it was given only for living in Canaan, given to teach this particular group of people how to live holy lives, then all the people born since need not bother with it, and the Law then belongs to the Jewish people alone. But Christians believe the Ten Commandments were given for all mankind for all times. These commands are, according to the apostle Paul, "our schoolmaster to bring us unto Christ" (Galatians 3:24 KJV). But once a person is brought to Christ, these laws are a rule of thumb for living that Christ Himself gives us the power to obey. It would not be fair to ask us to try to be perfect people if God didn't provide the help we needed for that. Christ Himself is the dynamic of all His demands in the person of the Holy Spirit.

Once the Spirit of God entered my life, I found myself using this new power inside me to change my whole way of thinking and living. I remember opening my mouth to speak a word that a young lady like me should not have even known, much less used! Suddenly there was a sort of inner check on my words. It was as if God said loudly and clearly, "No, Jill. Not now and not anymore. You shall not use My name in such a fashion."

I shut my mouth and whispered, "Sorry, Lord. Forgive me!"

"Done," I heard quite distinctly!

There was another reason Mr. Law was given to the Hebrew nation. God's people were expected to be both guardians of the truth and truth tellers. They were to be the missionary nation that said in glad surrender, "Here we are, Lord . . . send us!" They were about to enter the promised land and needed a God-given culture to make them distinct from the nations that didn't know God. So the Israelites were supposed to be a living picture of obedience to the laws of Mr. Law! They were to be a people who were deliciously, delightfully different, attracting inquiry as to the cause. So the rules they were given required obedience. Not only for their sake, but also for other people's sake.

We know from the Old Testament that that generation wandered around for forty years, and the people weren't obedient to the Law they were given. But because you are not obedient doesn't mean that God's Law is obsolete or that God's grace ceases or that God has changed His mind or made other plans for the human race. Knowing that His people would not graduate from Mr. Law's strict school of perfection, God still instructed them anyway and gave them great and precious promises.

God's school didn't include just the Ten Commandments either. There was so much more that the people needed to learn. The Law had basically two parts: first, the Ten Commandments, which you find in Exodus 20; and second, the ceremonial law or the ordinances that had to do with worship. I used to think that the Law was just the Ten Commandments. The Law is the Ten Commandments plus the ceremonial ordinances. You can read all of these in Exodus 21 through the books of Leviticus and Numbers.

GOD SET THE BAR HIGH

What was the point of it all? The Decalogue, or Ten Commandments, which we're considering at the moment, taught two things: the awesome holiness of God and the exceeding sinfulness of man. The ceremonial ordinances taught sinful man how to approach an outraged God, and how he could be forgiven and have a relationship with Him. The schoolmaster's first lesson was that it is a frightening, terrible thing for a sinner to fall into the hands of a holy God.

God revealed His holiness in His laws. A good God could not give bad laws. The Ten Commandments are good laws given by a good God. Only Somebody who was truly good and holy could think up these rules. They contained the highest standards, from the highest One. How else could it be?

Years later, God in Christ would walk this earth as a man and live up to every one of His own laws and ordinances. Jesus Christ would live with all the temptations that we face yet be without sin (Hebrews 4:15). He would show us the Law perfected.

Against that holy standard, the exceeding sinfulness of man showed up. The Law was given to show man that he had not measured up. That's why so many people hated Jesus. His sheer goodness was a rebuke to them. It made them feel guilty. His righteousness condemned them and made them feel bad about themselves.

IMPERFECTION IS SIN

Paul wrote that the Law is a "schoolmaster to bring us unto Christ" (Galatians 3:24 KJV). So if anybody asks you the reason for the Law, that's it, in a nutshell. The Law is the schoolmaster to bring you to Christ, who was the only One who was ever perfect.

The Law was not given to deliver us from the judgment of God because we think we've kept enough of it to pass the test! That's what the majority of people in many churches believe today, and they're wrong—dreadfully, terribly, terrifyingly wrong—because they are not going to go to heaven if they think they have kept enough of the Ten Commandments. Do you know why? Because it's impossible! If the only people who go to heaven are people who have kept the Ten Commandments, heaven is going to be empty! Man has never perfectly kept even a few of the Ten Commandments, yet people go on trying to do the best they can and hope it's good enough. But it isn't! Imperfection is sin.

One day I was in a luxury holiday resort. A very wealthy lady asked me, "How good do I have to be to go to heaven?"

"Perfect," I replied.

She looked at me, startled. "Then who can go?" she asked.

"Only those God forgives for their imperfection," I replied.

"And who would they be?" she pursued.

"Those who ask Him," I answered.

That's how it works. The Law shows us our imperfection; and if we ask in all sincerity, God forgives us for it.

The Law was given to show us we've come short of God's standard. It is a measuring stick that shows the exceeding sinfulness of man. Paul wrote, "All have sinned and fall short [of the standard] of the glory of God" (Romans 3:23). "All" means you and me. There is no exception, in case you thought you were it! Every single person on God's earth has come short of God's perfect standard. Even if you started today and kept every single one of the Ten Commandments for the rest of your life, what about all the ones you broke before you arrived at this state of perfection? You see, you haven't done it, I haven't done it, nor has anyone else!

THE REPORT CARD

If you aren't convinced you've gotten a failing grade from the schoolmaster, let's have a quick look at these commandments. Allow the Teacher of Righteousness to give you your report card.

I sometimes meet people who say, "I live by the Sermon

on the Mount, and I don't need that Christianity stuff." I try to point out that the Sermon on the Mount amplifies the Ten Commandments and makes them even harder to keep!

When we begin to talk to people who say, "I live by the Ten Commandments, but I can do it without God," we are talking with people who are breaking the first and greatest commandment of all. The first commandment is all about God being supreme. God says it's a big sin to ignore Him and think you are big enough and clever enough and good enough to live life well enough to please God and get to heaven on your own merits. That is saying to God that you are good enough without God. Independence is the essence of sin! The first commandment is, "You shall have no other gods before me" (Exodus 20:3). Trying to live life without reference to God is making yourself God.

Let's look at the next commandment. "You shall not make for yourself an image in the form of anything in heaven above or on the earth beneath" (v. 4). God was talking about idols that represent a spirit. God told us we mustn't worship spirits, yet today there are thousands of witches' covens in Britain alone, as well as in the United States and Canada, while Satan worship is openly practiced all over the world. And so this commandment is very relevant. There are people in our day and age who worship spirits, and they are not even bothering with the idols that represent them! They are ignoring God's revelation of Himself.

The sacredness of God's name must not be violated. The third commandment tells us that we are not to "misuse the name of the LORD [our] God" (v. 7). Some of us who work in business, or go to high school or college, know that blaspheming God's name seems to be the normal thing to do, yet God says that He "will not hold anyone guiltless who misuses his name" (v. 7). I think we need to be very careful. There are also derivations of God's name that Christians use all the time, such as *gosh* or *golly*. James the brother of Jesus warned, "Above all . . . do not swear—not by heaven or by earth or by anything else. All you need to say is a simple 'Yes' or 'No.' Otherwise you will be condemned" (James 5:12). Is the helper—the Holy Spirit—showing you that you have failed His exam? That you have come short of His standard?

Mr. Law talks about the sanctity of the Sabbath. "Remember the Sabbath day by keeping it holy" (Exodus 20:8; see also Isaiah 58:13–14). What do you do with your Sabbath? Do you follow your own pleasure instead of trying to please God on His holy day? Well, then, you've broken the Sabbath, according to the Scriptures. The Sabbath is for rest and spiritual enrichment. It is for delighting in the Lord.

What about the sanctity of the family, which is dealt with in the Ten Commandments? God commands the honor due to parents and the parents' responsibility for the children's behavior. God holds parents responsible for their children's attitudes to Him. That's a heavy thing. We are to bring our children to love and honor God and keep His Word. "Honor your father and your mother, so that you may live long in the land the LORD your God is giving you" (Exodus 20:12).

The sanctity of human life is also guarded by the commandment, "You shall not murder" (v. 13). Is this commandment kept? Millions of abortions kill babies worldwide. People are killing themselves with alcohol or drugs all over our nation today, and the sanctity of life is under fire.

The schoolmaster says that human life has value because we are made in the image of God. Today, people are not learning

Mr. Law's lessons—the sanctity of God's name, of the Sabbath, of the family, of marriage. None of these are the main concerns of human society today.

When Jesus came, He amplified Mr. Law's teachings. "You shall not commit adultery" (v. 14) was amplified in Matthew 5:28: "Anyone who looks at a woman lustfully has already committed adultery with her in his heart." Have you and I ever had one lustful thought or discovered porn on the Internet and have allowed ourselves to be captured by the image we saw and drawn into the habit? Then we have broken the Ten Commandments. The Bible teaches that if you have ever broken one of Mr. Law's laws, then you are guilty of breaking them all (James 2:10). Mr. Law is a perfectionist. Even if we get 99 on our exam paper, we need to know that the passing mark is 100, and we have all failed.

God told Mr. Law to teach us we mustn't steal or lie (Exodus 20:15–16). To do so violates the rights of our neighbor, and we are supposed to love our neighbor as ourselves. We mustn't covet "anything that belongs to [our] neighbor" (v. 17), including his house, his wife, his slaves, oxen, donkeys, or anything else he has. And so if anybody comes to me and says, "I live by the Ten Commandments," I tell that person, "Well, I'm very glad to meet you. You're the first person, apart from Jesus Christ, who ever has!"

The Law was given for a purpose, and it still has that purpose today. The Law is a schoolmaster to bring us to Christ, who can forgive us for breaking the Law and who alone has fulfilled the Law and can enable us to begin to obey the Law.

Mr. Law teaches that we have failed his class, have received an F on our report cards, and are in big trouble with God! The punishment of a failing grade is God's disapproval and condemnation (John 3:18).

But don't forget, there was another part of the Law given by God to Moses. That was the part called the ordinances. This ceremonial law was for those who acknowledged they had failed the course. Sinful man could bring a required offering and be forgiven. The offering was the unblemished lamb that bore the curse and the punishment for the one who brought it, as demanded by the Law. It was the man's substitute for judgment.

In Galatians 3:23–25, we read, "Before the coming of this faith [in Jesus Christ], we were held in custody under the law, locked up until the faith that was to come would be revealed. So the law was our guardian until Christ came that we might be justified by faith. Now that this faith has come, we are no longer under a guardian." True, we are no longer under the schoolmaster when we have left school, but we are expected to live out the lessons he taught us.

The Law will lead you to the living Lamb, who is Christ. He will impart to you the power to live the promised life in the promised land.

It's time to discover, discuss, and then apply the discoveries you have made. If you are using this for your own study time, record your findings in a notebook.

Summary

In a sentence or two, summarize what this chapter is about.

Discovery

1. Study the Ten Commandments, and remember that we are not under the Law but under grace. Grace is the means by which the power is made available for us to be law-abiding citizens of heaven while we are still on earth.

2. Read Exodus 20, Exodus 31:18, and Deuteronomy 5:22.
   a) How was the Law given? (Exodus 20:1.)
   b) To whom was it given? (Exodus 31:18.)

Discussion or Journal

1. "You shall have no other gods before me." Look up these related verses: Deuteronomy 6:5; 2 Kings 17:35; Jeremiah 24:7. How does God describe Himself in Exodus 20:5-6? How does this relate to us today?

2. Read Isaiah 43:1. Because of this fact, in all things God must have the preeminence (Colossians 1:18; Philippians 2:10-11). Paraphrase these verses in your own words.

3. What does God say the effects and results of spirit worship will be? If you are in a group, each look up a couple of these verses and share your findings: Exodus 32:33; Leviticus 19:31; 20:6; Isaiah 44:10-11; Exodus 20:5, 20; Jeremiah 25:8-11; Deuteronomy 5-9. Apply the verses to a modern situation.

4. "You shall not misuse the name of the LORD your God." Read Exodus 20:7; Leviticus 19:12; Matthew

5:33–37; 15:18–19; Colossians 3:8. Discuss how we should react in the workplace, school, or college situation to others casually blaspheming God's name.

Decision

1. What in this chapter most applies to you?
2. What do you need to do about it?
3. To summarize this study, write a paragraph on what your attitude should be to the Law.

Devotion

1. Pray through the discoveries you have made while reading this chapter.
2. Pray for these same discoveries for others.

A Personal Spiritual Workout

- *Day 1.* Read Exodus 20:8 and write a paragraph about your Sabbath. Be honest: Is it a joy or a bore? Why? What is forbidden in Scripture? (See Isaiah 58:13–14.) What is commanded? (See Exodus 20:8–11; 23:12; 31:13–16; Leviticus 23:3; Mark 3:4; Colossians 2:16; Luke 13:15–16.) Record in your notebook what you learn about Sabbath keeping.
- *Day 2.* What should you do if your father or mother tells you to do something wrong? Is it right to honor them and obey? (See Matthew 15:4; Ephesians 6:1–4; Colossians 3:20.) Or should you obey God rather

than man? (See Colossians 3:25; Acts 4:19; 5:29; Matthew 12:50.)

- *Day 3.* Look up Matthew 5:21; Mark 10:19; Luke 18:20. What is the root of the fruit of murder? What is the antidote for anger? (See 1 John 3:11, 15–16; Psalm 37:1–8; Ecclesiastes 7:9; Ephesians 4:26, 31–32.)
- *Day 4.* What should my Canaan marriage be like? What does God think of adultery? (See Leviticus 20:10; Ephesians 5:22–33; Hebrews 13:4; Mark 10:7–9.)
- *Day 5.* Look up Matthew 19:18; Mark 10:19; Romans 13:9. Is there anything you should make restitution for, now that you live in Canaan? (See Exodus 22:1, 3, 9.)
- *Day 6.* Write out Leviticus 19:18 and memorize it now. Look up Romans 12:19 as well.
- *Day 7.* Compare Romans 7:7 and 13:9. What is the antidote for covetousness? (See Romans 13:10; Luke 12:15.)

NINE

THE SACRED COW

Not only was Amalek in Canaan, but the Devil was there too. He must have swum across the Red Sea!

He obviously had not drowned along with the Egyptians. He was there, and he was waiting. He intended to challenge Israel every step of the way into the promised land. He intends to challenge you and me too! Having retired to lick his wounds over the fact that he has lost you, he will regroup and attack.

Essentially, Satan has one major goal. His aim in life has been, is, and will be to stop God's Word getting to the people. With this in mind, he busied himself in the Old Testament period planting seeds of disbelief and discontent in the minds of the children of Israel concerning Moses—God's mouthpiece—and God Himself.

Satan worked on drawing the Israelites' attention to their physical discomforts, knowing that if they muttered long enough and loud enough, they would not be able to hear God's voice.

However, he faced a new problem. So far, God's Law had been

given orally. Now, two huge stones were being engraved supernaturally on the mountain of God with the finger and the words of God, which would be the Devil's demise if obeyed. While Moses was on the mountain receiving those solid blocks of truth, the Devil went to work down in the valley, moving quickly before Moses reappeared with that indelible Rule Book. It is important to note his methods and learn how he operates (Exodus 32) so that we may recognize our Enemy and resist his temptations.

I WANT TO BE BIGGER

The Devil's first tactic was *delay*. "When the people saw that Moses was so long in coming down from the mountain, they gathered around Aaron and said, 'Come make us gods who will go before us. As for this fellow Moses who brought us up out of Egypt, we don't know what has happened to him'" (Exodus 32:1).

The Devil's devices haven't changed. Even as Christians, we tend to want everything right away, and the Devil takes full advantage of our impatience. "Give us everything now, if not sooner," we demand. Satan plays on that sign of immaturity. Who among us with small children is not familiar with the toddler's tantrums when his or her immediate needs aren't met? Kids won't wait.

Maybe you need to have a clear word from God concerning a decision you need to make. As Israel did, you camp at the foot of the mountain of God and wait for a voice from above. Should you take that job? Should you join that church? Should you date that person? Should you arrange for an aged parent to go into a retirement home?

You wait, but Moses—or whoever is God's human spokesman for you—is conspicuous by his absence. Perhaps you go to church on Sunday intent on listening carefully to your pastor. Maybe you will get the answer in the sermon. But nothing seems to be relevant to your dilemma, and you go home disappointed. So in your immaturity, you allow the Devil to stop the Word of God from getting to you. You will not wait! But you must learn that delay is all part of developing patience that develops maturity. As you wait, you are supposed to be growing up.

Stuart and I were visiting some old friends. They had four boys, and we hadn't seen them in a while. The older children were all chattering, while the smallest one, named Duncan, was trying to get a word in edgewise. His father noticed him.

"Duncan," he said, "tell Auntie Jill what you want to be when you grow up."

Overcome with the sudden attention, Duncan was quiet for a while. Then he brightened up and said, "I want to be bigger!"

We all laughed. We could understand his wanting. He wanted to be big enough to join in and not be treated as the youngest kid on the block.

Oh that you and I would want to grow up and "be bigger"! That we would determine that whatever method God saw fit to use to "grow us up" would indeed work to make us a spiritual adult. Always remember, when we want to know what God wants us to do or how God wants us to behave, He has prepared a word for us on the mountain. He has also prepared a right moment to deliver His word. He will not leave us uninformed.

If you are not sure what that word is, wait until you are sure. You don't need to ask, "Why the delay?" as a small child would ask. Grow up! God is in no hurry. He is testing you, wanting to know if you are willing to wait for your instructions, instead of running ahead of Him.

Whenever I am unsure of a way to act, or if I have a big decision to make and am not clear as to God's word about it, I meet with God at the mountain and settle down to wait. While I'm waiting, I read the Bible. I try to promise God I will wait until I read some principle or until I see some parallel to my situation in Scripture. Until I am sure I have God's permission, I dare not move away from the foot of the mountain.

In my experience, there have been many delays in my life. Sometimes I haven't known where to go for help to make the right move. Other times, God has had His own good, unrevealed reasons for leaving me in the dark. He has lessons for me to learn through the mystery of unanswered prayer. At such times I have tried not to let the Devil use delay to push me into impatient and ill-advised moves and unwise actions. That is what he wants to do; I don't have to oblige him!

Another tactic the Devil will use is *disillusionment*. It may be disillusionment with the human leader, as it was in our text. "As for this fellow Moses," I imagine the children of Israel said scathingly, "he used to lead us. Now he's off in a holy huddle on his religious mountain, and he's left us all behind." Maybe your Moses, who led you out of Egypt, seemed to lose interest in you and you were hurt. Perhaps your spiritual helper just disappeared out of your life. Or perhaps the life God seemed to promise you just didn't seem to be materializing, and in your heart you turned back to Egypt. This is exactly what the Bible says made these people sin and turn their hearts back to Egypt (Acts 7:39).

There seems to be a marked lack of respect in the way the Israelites were talking about their leaders. This should give us cause to think carefully before we gripe behind our leaders' backs. The next thing we know, our hearts will be looking longingly over our shoulders to "the good old days"!

What does it mean to turn back in our hearts? As far as the children of Israel were concerned, it meant deciding that other religions had something more to offer them than their "old-time religion." So they asked Aaron for gods like the Egyptians had. The Israelites did not reject the idea that they needed God; they simply began to accept other religious beliefs that had been part and parcel of their environment up until now. Those beliefs suddenly seemed as good, if not better, than their own.

A CARD-CARRYING CHRISTIAN

Turning back in our hearts may mean we quit going to church or meeting with other Christians. It could be we continue to go to church and do all the things we used to do as a card-carrying Christian, but our heart isn't in it and we secretly wish we didn't have to do it. Or we may find someone like Aaron who compromises his faith, too, and hang around with him.

Amazingly, Aaron acquiesced to the children of Israel's request to make an idol to worship. "Take off the gold earrings that your wives, your sons and your daughters are wearing, and bring them to me," he said (Exodus 32:2). "He took what they handed him" and fashioned the gold "into an idol cast in the shape of a calf." Then the leaders said to the people, "'These are your gods, Israel, who brought you up out of Egypt.' When Aaron saw this, he built an altar in front of the calf and announced, 'Tomorrow there will be a festival to the LORD'" (vv. 3–5). After this, the people went wild.

The problem with sin is you never just sin to yourself. If you go cold spiritually, you can lower the temperature of everyone else around you. I believe God will hold us accountable for that. God was angry with Aaron.

It could be that the people intimidated Aaron. He must also have been wondering what Moses was doing and if something had happened to him. However, there was no excuse for the easy collapse of his faith. And where was Miriam? She was a prophetess. She also considered herself called to speak on God's behalf to Israel, but we hear nothing from her at this critical point in time.

RELIGIOUS PROSTITUTION

In the commentary on Exodus 32:25, the Zondervan NIV Study Bible says: "The people had cast off all restraint; 'they were running wild and . . . out of control.' The exact word used twice in this verse *(pr')* is found in the warning of 'Where there is no revelation [i.e., message from or attention to the Word of God], the people cast off all moral restraints [i.e., they become ungovernable].'"

The idea of the verb "to cast off all restraint" is that of loosening or uncovering. It would appear that there was a type of religious prostitution connected with the people's worship of the golden calf. In the absence of a clear directive from the Lord through His appointed spokespeople, there is usually a loosening of morals and a lack of suitable behavior or worse. When Moses eventually came back, he realized that decisive action was required. So he challenged the people: "Whoever is for the

LORD, come to me" (Exodus 32:26). The Hebrew in translation literally is, "Whoever [is] for the LORD—to me!" (See also Joshua 24:14–15; 1 Kings 18:21; Matthew 6:24.)

It amazes me that the people did what Moses said! He must have had such authority and commanded enough respect to be heeded. His message was uncompromising. You are either on the Lord's side or you're not! There was a choice to make. God is God, or He is not! If God is who He says He is, the only right response is submission and obedience. Surrender to God's will and way. It really does matter.

Radical belief in God that gives away its life on a daily basis in order to let the whole world know about Him must be accompanied by a lifestyle that is morally pure. Tolerance for less than this has become the eleventh commandment. It is time for us to send out the call: "Whoever is for the Lord—to me!"

It is dreadfully possible to be a redeemed Christian, become sidetracked, and have our hearts turned aside by the "sacred cows" of man's speculative philosophies or religions. How many teenagers have enthusiastically committed their lives to Christ only to fall prey almost at once to syncretism? Maybe they looked to the established church to accept them, but older believers struggled with their appearance or lifestyle, and they fell prey to some modern sacred cow. The New Testament bears witness to this. Many wolves in sheep's clothing will be waiting for the appearance of new lambs on the scene. Even out-of-touch believers may trip up a young Christian trying to walk on the straight and narrow.

The Devil will be waiting for delay or disillusionment with established religion or traditional practices, and he will have a sacred cow in mind to take God's place. In this way, he will have achieved his desired result. He will have stopped the Word of God from building up the people and establishing them in the faith.

In the seventies, the Jesus Movement—a Christian revival among young people—was in full swing. Stuart and I were working among the many young hippie kids of the era. The church did not want to accept these "way-out" young people. They were concerned what the influence on their Christian children would be.

"Jill, get them cleaned up," I was told. "Then maybe we can welcome them." I struggled with this prejudice. These young-sters were coming to the Lord in droves, and I knew they needed to be in church so that the older believers could help us disciple them. But the church didn't want to disciple them! What's more, they didn't want them in their church pews dressed "like that." They didn't want their own kids mixing with them either!

I thought that the enthusiasm of the excited new converts might go a long way to do something about the boredom I had seen in the church kids. As I wondered what to do about the matter, a friend gave me some wise advice. "The oak tree has a lot of old leaves hanging all over its branches all winter," she said. "You can exhaust yourself if you like, climbing each tree and pulling off all the old leaves one by one, or you can just con-centrate on the new life, which is by far the easiest way. As the new life fills the tree, the old leaves drop off." I decided I would concentrate on training the new kids in studying the Bible and learning to pray. And as they did this the new life would fill the tree and the old leaves would drop off. This way, we let the new life of the Christ they had received do its own transforming work in their lives.

MAKING A SACRAMENT OF LIVING

Another way the Devil will try to achieve his ends may be to delight us out of delighting in God. He will suggest that all this trying to keep a set of rules will spoil all our fun. Why bother? Is it really worth it? The Devil says, "You shouldn't get so serious. Live a little. If Christianity is going to be a whole lot of 'Thou shalt nots,' it's not for you. It's just really a set of ten suggestions. It's not for everyone."

What you probably haven't realized is that the Devil has his own list of "Thou shalt nots." Do you remember that he said to Eve, "You will not certainly die" (Genesis 3:4)? That was a downright lie! Adam and Eve did die as a result of eating the forbidden fruit. The difference between the Devil's "Thou shalt nots" and God's is that the Devil's list is full of lies, while God's list is full of truths. Satan's lies bring death and suffering, while God's truth brings life and joy.

The Devil advised the children of Israel, "Enjoy yourselves. Live it up. Eat, drink, and be merry. Moses isn't coming back." Aaron, who knew better, did not interfere. In fact, incredibly, he aided and abetted them. The people "sat down to eat and drink, and rose up to play" (Exodus 32:6 NKJV). "Thou shalt not be so serious-minded," Satan said. "Enjoy thyself." The Israelites complied.

God wants us to enjoy ourselves, but He knows there is a time and place for it and a proper way to do it (Ecclesiastes 3:1–8). "There is nothing better for a man than that he should eat and drink, and find enjoyment in his toil. This also, I saw, is from the hand of God" (Ecclesiastes 2:24 RSV). We are supposed to offer all our work and ordinary things to God for His glory.

"So whether you eat or drink or whatever you do, do it all for the glory of God" (1 Corinthians 10:31). In other words, we are to make no distinction between the secular and the sacred. We are to make a sacrament of living. It is all to be done in God and for God.

God also knows that the Devil lies when he suggests he can give us a good time. Maybe we shall choose to enjoy the pleasures of sin for a season, but as we have already seen, Moses had enough spiritual sense to know the season lasts a very short time. This was not the time or place for Israel to have a pleasure party for a sacred cow! But the Devil succeeded in distracting them from waiting on God. He told them a terrible lie. He said that play was more important than prayer, while hiding the fact that playing with God's rules leads to plagues. "The Lord struck the Israelites with a plague because of what they did with the calf" (Exodus 32:35). You cannot play the fool with God and get away with it. God's "Thou shalt nots" are given by a good God who wants us to enjoy all His goodness. They are given to protect our joy, not rob us of it. The Devil's lies lead to the destruction of our very lives.

God wants us to make a sacrament of living. He wants us to be obedient children when our leaders are out of sight and not compromise our faith when delay or disillusionment come along.

After Moses came down from the mountain and dealt with the Israelites, they repented. Exodus 33:4–6 states that the people *mourned* and stripped themselves of their ornaments. They flung away similar articles they had given Aaron to worship the calf (v. 2) as they realized the Devil's lie and understood they should have waited on God as He told them to. They should not have allowed themselves to be distracted.

They should have delighted in God and not so soon substituted a calf for the God who had worked such wonders in their lives and brought them out of Egypt.

So Satan will use the illusion of delight without devotion, fun, play, or even the very normal things in life like eating and drinking to prevent the Word of God getting to the people.

The Devil brought them to *depravity*. Look at Exodus 32:25: The people were "running wild." The King James Version says that they were "naked." How far away can you get from God's laws of purity and modesty? Even their enemies would hear of it and be disgusted. "Aaron had let them get out of control and so become a laughingstock to their enemies" (v. 25). It's possible to live in Canaan and sink as low as this. To our shame, non-Christians may have higher standards of morality than we do!

You can find redeemed men and women leaping around at parties without their clothes on, while even their enemies (who are at the party too) reject that sort of behavior. It's happening today, and it's one sure way the Devil will use to stop the Word of God getting to the people. Which people? The enemies who are watching and whom God wants to convert into His friends.

BREAKING THE TEN COMMANDMENTS

Lastly, the Devil will use *despair*. When Moses came down from the mountain and saw what was happening, he literally broke the Ten Commandments! He had God's Rule Book in his hands to present to the people. But even Moses threw his golden opportunity away. When Moses saw what the children of Israel were doing, he allowed Amalek to triumph over him.

His old anger burned as the Devil furiously fanned the flame, and throwing the tablets of stone out of his hands, *he* broke the Law! Literally! Satan achieved his desired end. He delayed the Word of God from getting to the people.

How many ministers leave the ministry each year? How many missionaries return home? How many Christian deacons and elders resign from office, throwing away their opportunity to get the Word of God to the people? They don't always throw it away because they can't believe it or because they do not live by it, but because sometimes, like Moses, they are overcome with anger and despair. If they leave their murmuring, muttering congregation alone for even a short space of time, what happens? Disobedience, disillusionment, depravity, and despair. If the Devil can, he will. Will what? Anyhow, any way, anytime, stop the Word of God getting to the people! He'll attack the listeners, and he'll attack the messengers of the truth that sets men and women free.

Stuart and I travel the world as we respond to invitations to train church leaders and encourage missionaries on the field. One of the most common things we deal with is discouragement. God's servants become discouraged in some way or another, and the defeated grow so despondent they return from the field or quit the church. It can be temper you struggle with, as Moses apparently did. It can be compromise because someone intimidates you. It can be lack of trust that God will come through for you. Whatever it is, you need to know that we might—in fact we will—break the Ten Commandments along the way, but if so, God is there with forgiveness and strength to turn us around and encourage us to get on with the journey, for God is determined to make us determined!

GOD IS DETERMINED

There is one fantastic thing about this narrative in Exodus 32. It is a word also beginning with *D*, and it has to do with God. It is the word *determination*. The Devil is busy, but God is busier and determined to speak and to work with those who will listen. Though men or women may ignore, disobey, or break His Word, it does not alter the truth or the worth of it. It doesn't dissipate the power of it. The written Word is a living Word abiding forever. God used a word to tell Abraham, Isaac, and Jacob that He would bring them into the promised land (Exodus 33:1), and because God stands behind His promises, He would not let the Devil, His chosen people, or even His chosen leaders frustrate His purposes.

God would find some who believed. He would bring in those who, like Caleb, wholly followed Him and, like Joshua, would stake their lives on His Word. Only two of that generation were undefeated. The rest never made it into the promised land because of disobedience—Moses, Aaron, and Miriam included.

But two obedient followers were sufficient for God, and the Devil could not stop them. And even the example of the unbelief of their parents could not prevent the children of the children of Israel from entering in. The Law would be written again on new tablets of stone and pronounced afresh to the people. The schoolmaster would set up school again, and the pupils would have a chance to enroll. No matter how brightly the sacred cow had glistened, it would not be allowed to blind the few who would hear, believe, and decide to be on the Lord's side.

To be on the Lord's side means you will be dedicated to waiting for the Word, whatever the delay, disillusionment, depravity, or despair you find in your soul or in other people. To be on the Lord's side means you will be determined to deliver the Word to the people to whom He sends you.

It's time to decide whose side you are on. Try to imagine yourself standing in front of a furious Moses who has just made you drink the bitterness of your actions. If you have failed, as Israel and Aaron failed, then repent. Tell God you're sorry. Climb Sinai one more time, and let God chisel out His laws on the tablet of your heart. Then, as Moses did in Exodus 34, carry it down to the people and share it with them!

It's time to discover, discuss, and then apply the discoveries you have made. If you are using this for your own study time, record your findings in a notebook.

Summary

In a sentence or two, summarize what this chapter is about.

Discovery

1. Recap and discuss the following ways the Devil tries to prevent the Word of God from getting to the people:
   a) Delay, disillusionment, depravity, and despair.
   b) Share any personal illustrations you can think of to demonstrate these points.

Discussion or Journal

1. The sacred cow illustrates the glistening lure of different beliefs. Look up the following verses, and make a list of the ways we can help ourselves recognize an invitation, even by an Aaron, to "set up other gods to go before us" (Exodus 32:1).

    a) Read 2 Timothy 3:13–17. What is the warning here? What is the exhortation?

    b) Read 1 John 4:1–4. The "little children" are warned about the false prophets. How can we test their message? Discuss verses 2 and 3. Who will help us to overcome them?

    c) Read 2 Peter 2:1–3. Describe how these false teachers will work. List the words that describe their methods.

Decision

1. What in this chapter most applies to me? What do I need to do about it?

2. As teachers of God's truth, we are instructed how to act. Not as Moses did—reacting in anger—but according to 2 Timothy 2:24–26. Read these verses and pray about this.

Devotion

1. Even when the people you teach refuse to listen (2 Timothy 4:3–4), you have your orders as a disciple of Jesus to minister the gospel (v. 5). Write out verse 5 in capital letters and memorize it.

2. It would be a good idea to read some small concise work on cults and other religions. I recommend Dr. Walter Martin's books and recordings for study and reference.

If you spend too much time studying error, you can get more confused. Rather, give priority to study of the truth and you will learn to discern error. I have heard that the employees of banks are given a period of practice handling and studying real money so that they learn to spot the counterfeit; it works the same way for faith.

A Personal Spiritual Workout

Each day choose a thought or look up a verse in your notes pertaining to the lessons learned, and *meditate* (which means to "chew it over") throughout the day. Pray about it each night.

TEN

RESTRAINED
FROM BRINGING

Having taught Israel the way they should live, God began to instruct them in the way they should worship (Exodus 35:1–36:7). On the mountain, God gave Moses explicit instructions about the construction of a house for God to dwell in. God promised to come and tabernacle (or make his home) among the Israelites, making His glory visible. Can you imagine how this would have encouraged the people?

The house that was to be built could not possibly contain all of God, for as Solomon prayed in his dedication prayer, "Will God really dwell on earth? The heavens, even the highest heaven, cannot contain you. How much less this temple I have built!" (1 Kings 8:27). God doesn't dwell in places made with hands (Acts 7:48; 17:24). Yet He deigned to meet with Israel in person, in an earthly structure made according to His own design (Hebrews 8:5). In the tabernacle, Israel worshipped God.

WORSHIP AND WORK GO TOGETHER

Work and worship must go together. *Worship* means attributing worth to a person—giving honor where it's due. As we come to know and understand the Person we attribute worth to, we, though crippled with wrongdoing, will be led to lean hard on His arm and be shown how to walk in newness of life. The natural end that our thankful hearts should have for all of God's redemptive work for us is worship. But worship is not merely gazing up at heaven, dewy eyed. Part of worship is work. It's wonderful to worship, but it doesn't stop when we go to work.

If to worship God means to spend time acknowledging His worth, then it follows He is worth doing things for. This is also a form of worship. If only we could get across to the church the fact that worship incorporates work, we would find ourselves in the same gloriously embarrassing position of the folks in charge of building the tabernacle. We would need to restrain the people "from bringing" (Exodus 36:6).

Can you just imagine having a building program at your church, passing the plate, and finding you had enough for what you need halfway into the offering? Can you imagine the usher going discreetly to the minister and whispering in his ear, "Please tell them not to give any more—we have more than enough." I wish!

PRACTICAL WORSHIP

Moses had been up the mountain and received a pattern, or blueprint, for the building of this huge church in the wilderness. After Moses reported everything God told him about the tabernacle to the people, the time had come for a response from them. The response was quite overwhelming. It wasn't a question of squeezing a dollar or two out of a few reluctant people. God told them what was needed, and the children of Israel matched their possessions and abilities to the needs of the church. That's worship! (Read Exodus 36:1–7.)

Too many people today think that worship is singing in the choir or preaching or teaching. They believe worship is a passive or active exercise, but definitely a spiritual thing. I believe that practical service *is* spiritual worship.

There's an apocryphal story told of Jesus going back to heaven and being asked by the angels, "Whom did you entrust with the message of salvation?" Jesus pointed out big old Peter busy putting his foot in his mouth, James and John having their usual Sons-of-Thunder row, Thomas running around doubting everybody and everything, and Andrew tied up in a knot of inadequacy. "I've left it with them," He said simply. "But Master," the angels said, aghast, "what happens if they fail?" Jesus replied, "I have no other plans!"

GIVE US THE TOOLS AND WE'LL FINISH THE JOB

I was born six years before World War II began, and I can remember Winston Churchill asking the United States for help. We in Britain were fighting the war with almost our bare hands! No one can win a battle without weapons, and no one would expect anyone to! Churchill said, "Give us the tools and we'll finish the job." America responded.

God has given us tools to "finish the job." A war greater than any earthly conflict has engulfed the world. It is the war between good and evil. God knows we need weapons to fight with, and He has responded. What is more, "The one who calls you is faithful, and he will do it" (1 Thessalonians 5:24). Apart from the weapons of our warfare mentioned in Ephesians 5, God equipped us with our natural abilities and with the empowering Holy Spirit, who gifted us with spiritual abilities as well. Every good and perfect gift is from God (James 1:17).

First of all, we must realize that natural talents are not necessarily spiritual gifts. Many unbelievers are wonderfully talented people. But no unbeliever is spiritually gifted, because you can't be spiritually gifted without the Holy Spirit. Can spiritual gifts be practical? Yes, but before I confuse you, let us simply look at our text and confine ourselves to what we can learn from Exodus 35 about the tools we have been given to worship God.

A WILLING HEART

We can all agree that an offering is a religious, spiritual sort of thing. Right? Well, right and wrong. The worship God asked from His people at this point was a work offering. Let's look at how the offering was to be offered. The how of worship was very simple. The people were to offer whatever they brought with a willing heart. The people were told their offering was to be voluntary, not compulsory. "Everyone who is willing is to bring the Lord an offering" (Exodus 35:5). God has much to say on this point. Paul told us not to give grudgingly or of necessity, but hilariously, for God loves a hilarious giver (2 Corinthians 9:7).

What parent doesn't understand this? How often do you ask your youngsters for some service and decide to do without it when met with a sullen face? Oh, what joy to receive a cheerful, "Sure, Mom!" A willing heart is worth the entire world, isn't it? Sitting in a pew, because there's no way out of it, isn't worship. And doing a job around the church is only worship if done cheerfully and with a willing heart. That's an offering God asks for and will accept. Over and over again, God asks for those with willing hearts to worship Him with their work; and part of that work is the attitude that accompanies it.

WHAT ARE YOU GOOD AT DOING?

Consider also what the Israelites gave. They gave according to their natural abilities, but notice their natural abilities had been polished and disciplined until they were like fine instruments, ready for the surgeon's hand. The Living Bible paraphrases it this way: "Come, all of you who are skilled craftsmen having special talents, and construct what God has commanded us" (Exodus 35:10 TLB).

God gives each of us talents. They are like raw material hidden in a mountainside; gems buried under fauna. We must dig up those hidden properties we find in the earth of our lives and begin to polish and shape them for display and use. When they are ready, we can bring them voluntarily to God as an offering and ask Him where He wants these gems set. This is exactly what the people did. Those who could weave did so and brought the finished product; those who could carve wood presented their craftsmanship. Those who had no such talent but had strong arms and healthy bodies offered to carry and haul the heavy materials into place. Those who had abilities to work precious metals set them apart for the service of the Lord.

Stop a moment and think of your natural talents. What are you better at than anything else? What are you good at and what do you enjoy doing? What practical work is very easy and natural for you to do? Have you ever dedicated that work to God and realized that He considers it just as much an offering of worship as some spiritual ability?

When I first came to Christ, I remember someone telling me I needed to dedicate, or set apart, my natural abilities for God's service. If I really thought God was worth it, then He should have the use of those things He had gifted me with in the first place. I made a list. There were my tennis and ice-skating abilities. Whatever was God going to do with those? Then there was my artistic ability, and I did love writing letters to friends, so I put that down. I had no way of knowing at the time that the practice I would have in those directions would lead into writing Christian books and running sports programs for teenagers.

I thought about my love of dramatic art. All these were things I was good at and certainly enjoyed doing before I knew Jesus. Things I had brought out of Egypt with me, like the children of Israel had brought those jewels and materials with them into the promised land. I knelt down and gave them all to God and told Him that if He could use them, He was welcome! He did, and He has been ever since.

Tennis is a popular sport in England, and God gave me the idea of inviting my unbelieving friends to play tennis with me and using the opportunity to share Christ with them. I began to reach many people with my tennis racket! Winning souls at the tennis club was far more thrilling than winning tennis tournaments. I've done both, so I can testify to that.

I gave God my artistic and dramatic abilities, too, and immediately found use for them in creating a play we used on the streets and coffee bars of Europe to meet and reach unchurched kids. When I became a pastor's wife in an American church, I wrote and produced musical dramas that combined hundreds of talents and gifts from our congregation. I have yet to use my ice-skating ability, but maybe one of these days we'll do that art-and-drama play on ice in one of the shopping malls with an ice rink. Why not? Imagine the audience that would gather for that one.

A friend of mine brought her creative art abilities to Jesus, and now she teaches six art classes, all involving sharing her testimony. She also has the opportunity to go to social clubs, taking her art and drawing and applying spiritual parallels from her painting.

Worship involves bringing a willing offering of our natural abilities, and when we have worked to polish and discipline them, God will put our talents to work for Him. He will also give us certain detailed instructions about where and how to use them. The details given in Exodus 36 were minute. It was absolutely clear where each talent needed to be used. Can you sew? Sew for Jesus. Can you landscape? Ask Him where, when, and how. What gift did you bring with you from Egypt to Canaan? Will you worship Jesus with it right now?

So when do we begin? When do we bring our talents to the Lord? The answer is every day! "Moses gave them the materials donated by the people of Israel as sacred offerings for the completion of the sanctuary" (v. 3 NLT). So bring your talents and work every day, until God tells you to stop. Not just on Sundays—we must be more creative than that. When your church has got too much of everything and there is no more room for you or your talents, then you can have a rest.

TALENTS FOR THE TIME

Some people are talented in many areas. Perhaps we need to spend a season in prayer and ask God which specific talents He wants us to polish and use for a particular time, and which ones He wants us to lay aside for a time. God was more specific in His instructions to Moses to bring exactly those things that were required *at that time* for the building of the tabernacle. Later, other gifts were needed, such as musical, technical, and maintenance abilities. When we have dedicated ourselves to God, then it follows He is the One who guides us to certain areas of service at specific times. At one time in Stuart's life, he used his musical talent in a singing group; then he laid that aside for mathematical talent needed to keep the accounts of a missionary society. A few years ago, my creative art and craft abilities were tested to the fullest, putting together a nursery school with very few funds. This school was to be an outreach to the city. It had to pass stringent government requirements to be registered, and it was to be held in an old and broken-down warehouse we bought, with dead dogs and rats in the basement. We needed lots of practical talent!

I begged ends of wooden planks from lumberyards and cut, polished, and painted pictures on them for building blocks. We made paints from powders and dyes. Creating water troughs and sand trays was easy, but creating musical instruments was more difficult. Amazingly, we created an entire band from metal coat hangers, empty bottles, tin cans, and beans!

Our nursery school not only was passed by the authorities, but it became *the* place to send children. I remember well talking a brewer into letting me have his empty beer barrels, which we cut in half for tables, and making a climbing apparatus from the local tire junkyard. I loved every minute of that six-month endeavor, and God used my practical talents to begin a venture that served thousands of children over thirty years and paid the salaries of many missionaries. Since then, God has not asked me to use those particular talents, but they are stored away ready to be used if He ever needs them again. The willingness to be available and directed by God is what is important. To take up or lay down whichever tool He asks for, when He asks for it. But we don't just need direction; we need supernatural help. We need the filling of the Spirit to accomplish all tasks for God.

It's interesting to see what the Bible says about the man God called to supervise and teach others these practical crafts for the building of the tabernacle. Exodus 35:31 states that God filled Bezalel with His Spirit for "all kinds of skills." When we recognize that our practical abilities are gifts from God and dedicate them willingly to Him, He will fill us with His Spirit, who will impart to us the know-how to worship Him with our skills. So a Spirit-filled person is not just a person who prays, preaches, or witnesses for Christ, but one whose workmanship is the vehicle for God's power and usefulness as well. The Bible also teaches that along with our practical talents, the Holy Spirit gifts us with spiritual abilities. These are imparted to us and may or may not be meshed along the same talent lines we have been talking about. Someone never formally trained in education may discover he or she has a real gift as a teacher of the Scriptures. Then again, someone trained as a schoolteacher may experience a touch of God on Bible teaching and realize his or her spiritual gift runs along the line of his or her trained natural talent.

The spiritual gifts God gives are for encouraging and building up the body of believers spiritually. They are used for enlisting, enabling, enriching, and encouraging others. The apostle Paul wrote of special gifts for church office, ministry, and outreach to those outside the body of Christ (1 Corinthians 12:1–11).

SEE IF YOU CAN
RECOGNIZE YOUR GIFT

Look at this list of definitions of the special gifts for Christian ministry that may help you to identify the gift God has given to you to exercise. Keep in mind as you read the list that gifts require careful identification.

1. Specific gifts for church office (1 Corinthians 12:28–30; Romans 12; Ephesians 4):
   a. Apostles—purifiers of doctrine, pioneers
   b. Prophets—forthtellers and foretellers of truth
   c. Teachers—instructors
   d. Evangelists—traveling presenters of the gospel
   e. Pastors—overseers of congregations
   f. Rulers—those who "stand before"
2. Special gifts for Christian ministry:
   a. Word of wisdom—ability to explain the deep things of God

b. Word of knowledge—ability to receive a special understanding or intuition from God

c. Faith—ability to believe God when others are floundering

d. Healing—ability to convey God's sovereign healing touch

e. Miracles—ability to be involved with God in doing works of power

f. Prophecy—ability to forthtell and foretell truth

g. Discerner of spirits—ability to evaluate spiritual profession and ministry

h. Tongues—ability to speak in unknown languages

i. Interpretation—ability to interpret tongues

j. Exhortation—ability to encourage

k. Helpers—ability to be supportive

l. Acts of mercy—ability to serve others in a cheerful manner, kind and compassionate too

Our spiritual gifts need finding, using, and training in the same way as our practical talents. But we need to be careful not to get more enamored with the gifts than with the Giver of those gifts.

When Stuart used to travel extensively, he would come home to a very excited wife and three equally excited children. Once our children ran to him, asking, "What did you bring us, Daddy?" It was a childish question that was easy to understand and forgive. However, if I had met my husband with the same question, Stuart would probably have been justifiably hurt. We need to be adult enough to want the Giver of gifts more than those things he brings us!

The Corinthian church had become supremely gift-conscious, to the exclusion of being God-conscious. We must remember that the gifts of the Spirit are not as important as the fruit. As Paul warned in 1 Corinthians 13, we may speak with the tongues of men or angels, but if our gifts are not exercised in love, we gain nothing at all. A missionary may be marvelously talented and richly gifted spiritually but have no self-control. This can lead to total disaster in his relationships with the very people he has traveled thousands of miles and spent many years training to reach.

As far as I can see from Exodus 36, the key is a heart presented to God, in whose hands it is filled with wisdom and stirred to work for Him (v. 2). Then it is a matter of obedience to God's commands. "So Bezalel, Oholiab, and every skilled person to whom the LORD has given skill and ability to know how to carry out all the work of constructing the sanctuary are to do the work just as the LORD has commanded" (v. 1).

When the heart is willingly given, then the rest will follow and the leaders of our churches will hear the glad news Moses heard: "'The people are bringing more than enough for doing the work the LORD commanded to be done.' . . . So the people were restrained from bringing more, because what they already had was more than enough to do all the work" (vv. 5–7).

The King James Bible says, "the stuff they had was sufficient for all the work to make it, and too much."

Can you imagine such a thing happening today? Let me ask you a question. Would you say this is a description of your industry for the Lord? Is the "stuff" you are practically producing too much? Is someone going to have to restrain you from bringing? Or are you dwelling in your paneled houses while God's house lies in waste (Haggai 1:4)? This is a very challenging question for me, and I would hope it is a challenging question for you too.

It's time to discover, discuss, and then apply the discoveries you have made. If you are using this for your own study time, record your findings in a notebook.

Summary

In a sentence or two, summarize what this chapter is about.

Discovery

1. Read 2 Corinthians 9:7 and Exodus 35:10. What were the two things God was looking for? How does this give you a clue as to your responsibility concerning your talents and how to use them?

2. If talents are natural abilities given by God, take a minute and think of yours. What are you naturally good at? What do you get *A*'s for? What do you enjoy doing outside school hours, home time, or work, for which you have certain ability?

Discussion or Journal

1. If you are in a group, each person should share the one natural talent (not spiritual gift) that you think is your best. If you are having trouble, let your friends help you out. If you are on your own, make a list and discuss it with your pastor.

2. Read Exodus 35:20–29. Where did the people find the gifts they brought? Would it have required time or cost them effort to give them? Why? Who were the two men God called to head the work (vv. 30, 34)?

3. Make a list from verses 31–35 of fourteen things the Spirit of God did with their talents. Exodus 36:1 states that the Eternal gave the know-how for these practical abilities. Do you see how practical talents can be an acceptable offering to God's work in the church? Discuss.

4. Read Matthew 25:31–36. Where else must our practical talents be used? Share in the group what practical skills are needed for outreach to the lost (see vv. 35–36).

5. If you are a teenager, ask yourself how you can be preparing to be useful in your adult life. If you are an adult, discuss how you can begin to practice your skills.

Decision

1. Look up the following verses on being faithful with our God-given talents, and write down what you learn. Keep in mind that to be faithful means to be trusted. Answer one of these questions each day this week.

   a) Who is our Great Example (Hebrews 3:1–2)?

   b) Where was Moses faithful (Numbers 12:7)?

   c) The writer of Proverbs 25:13 tells us another

time we must be faithful. When is it, and to whom must we be faithful?

d) God has a promise for the faithful here. What do you think it is (Proverbs 28:20)?

e) How many things do we need practice in being faithful (Matthew 25:21)? Where do we start?

f) Read Daniel 6:1-5. In what practical areas was Daniel faithful?

g) What does Luke 16:10 mean? How can we apply this to ourselves?

Devotion

Complete one of the following each day.

1. Read 1 Corinthians 12. What illustration does the apostle Paul use to show the different gifts (v. 12)?

2. Write down and pray about twelve things you can learn about gifts from verses 4-27.

3. Read 1 Corinthians 13:1-3. Are the *fruits* of the Spirit or the *gifts* of the Spirit more important? Why?

4. The fruits of the Spirit are found in Galatians 5:22-23. Look this up and pray about the fact that these would be more important in a missionary's life than gifts.

5. Think about the list of gifts of ministry. Do you recognize any of your own? Are you active in practicing your gifts? Pray about it.

6. Pray that all the people in your church who have practical gifts to offer would offer them.

7. Pray for those who need affirmation in these areas. Ask yourself, "Could I give them affirmation?"

A Personal Spiritual Workout

Each day choose a thought or look up a verse in your notes pertaining to the lessons learned and *meditate* (which means to "chew it over") throughout the day. Pray about it each night.

ELEVEN

THE TABERNACLE

Many books have been written about the tabernacle. I have loved each lecture and illustration about this subject, so it is hard to approach the many chapters that have been so well plowed over and seek to drive yet another furrow. But I will take up the task.

Not too long ago, during a visit to Jordan, a friend took us into the desert where a model of the tabernacle—built to size—stood in the searing sun. Churches in America have built this replica as a tourist attraction. It is quite wonderful! Because of the troubles in the Middle East, we were the only visitors.

Many things surprised me, delighted me, and overwhelmed me as we had our tour and explanation with all the time in the world to ask our questions and try to put ourselves back thousands of years to Exodus days. We were all busy with our own wonderings, trying to imagine what this place meant to the children of Israel. But that would just have been an academic exercise. I had to walk back in thought to the present era and ask, "What does it mean to me today?" Can the symbolism and the pictures and this amazing visual aid God drew for the human race in the sands of time speak to, help, and instruct us now in the twenty-first century? The answer is a resounding yes!

The book of Hebrews uses the pictures and lessons of the tabernacle to apply parallels for the church and the believer today. The writer spoke about one's relationship to God, about the work of the Lord Jesus Christ, and about the precious promises of a life lived in the depths of the soul, where God abides. So what are the lessons we can learn from the tabernacle, and how can we apply them to the Christian life? This is not just about prayer and worship. If it were, some of us with other spiritual interests might be tempted to say, "Here am I, Lord . . . please send a member of the prayer team!" No, this is for every single one of us who counts Jesus precious.

Before we go inside the tabernacle, we need to take note of the position of the whole structure. The tabernacle was positioned in the very center of the camp. It took center stage—symbolic of the fact that God must be in the very center of our lives. He must take pride of place in our national life and our personal life. Having the tabernacle in such a position also meant that it could be protected. It doesn't take too much thought to realize we must protect our relationship with God above all things. He must always have the preeminence. He must be the pride of my life, the centrifugal force of all my living and all my doing. He must be in the center of the camp! So there was meaning in the position of the tabernacle. Everyone who saw it understood where God expected His people to place Him.

God also had a plan in the structure of the tabernacle. There was the outer part where you entered, the inner part where the priests worked, and the inner sanctum called the holy of holies, where only the high priest was allowed once a year on the Day of Atonement, and never without blood!

In Hebrews 9:11–15, the writer talked about how Jesus, our great High Priest, did not enter the holiest heaven with the blood of goats or bulls, but with His own blood. There through the eternal Spirit He offered himself once for all mankind. All the pictures of the Day of Atonement were brought to fruition on the cross.

The high priests in the Old Testament would enter with the spotless lamb, and the lamb's blood would be shed in order that the people could be forgiven. The high priest would then mediate for the people. Verse 15 says, "For this reason Christ is the mediator of a new covenant, that those who are called may receive the promised eternal inheritance—now that he has died as a ransom to set them free from the sins committed under the first covenant."

So Christ didn't enter an earthly tabernacle "that was only a copy of the true one; he entered heaven itself, now to appear for us in God's presence" (v. 24). This is God's pattern for us to enjoy God's present presence. He has opened "a new and living way" for you and for me (Hebrews 10:20).

How much time do we spend in the holy of holies? There are those who enter the outer court of a worship walk with God and stay there; those who, like the priests, continue on into the holy place; and those who somehow live in "the Holiest of all," as the King James Version so beautifully calls that most intimate of places (Hebrews 9:3). The holiest of all was the living quarters of God Himself, the place where the very presence of God was continuously manifested. As New Testament Christians, our position is clear. Unlike Israel in the wilderness, a way has been made by Jesus to enable us to freely walk into the holiest of all whenever we will. What an incredible privilege. There is a place inside our souls where God lives.

God, in the person of His Spirit, now lives in the tabernacle of our souls. He wants to make His presence known not only to us, but to all who pass by. The more time we spend in conscious enjoyment of God, the more everyone will sense His presence in our lives.

FIRST THINGS FIRST

We should never take advantage of God's grace. We all too often say, "Here am I, Lord . . . I'll come when I'm ready," or "I'll come if I like," or "I'll come when I've nothing else to do." I believe it is God's intention that every believer live out his life in the holiest of all every moment of every day, as well as benefiting from worship in every part of the tabernacle in every dimension.

I believe with all my heart that our Lord Jesus has made the way into the holiest of all, and you and I may enter into all that has been made available to us. So let us look at this marvelous visual aid the Father built for His children in the sands of their wanderings.

With the tabernacle set up in the very center of camp, the tribes were told to position themselves around it, each in their given place. The structure where God would live among them had to be in the midst, and so it must be with us: God central, with all we have and are gathered around Him. God is not to be moved off to the circumference, but He must take pride of place in our national, social, and personal lives.

The first time the tabernacle was erected, it was easy for

the people to do it all just right (Exodus 40). What excitement, what a thrill! What a new and unique experience. But then the journey began. Every time there was a move by that huge congregation, everything had to be packed up in a prescribed way and carried to the next resting place. Sometimes they stayed only a few days in one spot. How tempting it must have been not to bother setting it up at all. Or how easy it would have been for them to throw the thing together at the outer ring of the camp and just fellowship together instead.

Every single time they moved, the people had to decide to set God in the center so that, in case of attack by their enemies, the sacred things could be guarded. We do not watch the holy things God has entrusted to us carefully enough. So often we are guilty of carelessly leaving the things concerning our God scattered in all directions around the outskirts of our camp.

The Christian life is a series of choices that take place every day. Every morning when we get up, we need to ask ourselves: Have I set up the tabernacle? Today is it in the very center of my life? Is everything in place before I journey into my day? Have I attended to first things first? So the position, purpose, and plan of the tabernacle were explained to the people of God.

SYMBOLS OF SIGNIFICANCE

Many marvelous parallels can be drawn from the tabernacle. The book of Hebrews explains a lot of it for us. The whole structure instructs us so much about the person of the Lord Jesus Christ, our great High Priest who lives within to minister to us, that it pays to take a closer look at some of the details. As soon as we decide to allow God to be in the center of our lives, and we have come through the narrow gate "that leads to life" (Matthew 7:14), we enter into our first worship experience with God.

As soon as we begin to worship, we, like our friends in the wilderness, are confronted with the brazen altar, where the continually burning sacrifice glows. We, like they, will need to be reminded that a Lamb has been slain and a life given. That brazen altar was a continual reminder to those pilgrims, and I, too, need some symbols to remind me of Christ's sacrifice.

That is why the Lord's Supper is so important. The broken bread and poured-out wine remind us that "without the shedding of blood there is no forgiveness" (Hebrews 9:22).

Christians need to come to the Lord's Table regularly, just as the people in Exodus days needed to come to the brazen altar regularly. They would bring their lamb and lay their hands upon its head, and then the lamb would be killed. It was their "at-onement" with God. When we come to the Lord's Table, we can look back to the day when we, by faith, placed our hands on the Lamb of God and imputed our sin to our Substitute. "Do this in remembrance of me," Jesus said (Luke 22:19), and in remembering Him, we are reminded of the price of our redemption and what has been accomplished for us.

YOUR RELATIONSHIP DEPENDS UPON YOUR BIRTH, BUT YOUR FELLOWSHIP UPON YOUR BEHAVIOR

Next, the people in Exodus days came to the laver of cleansing. This was where a ceremony of foot washing took place. In the outer court of our first worship experiences with God, we have to learn that our feet need to be continually cleaned. We get so dirty walking around this world, and daily we need Him to take our feet, just as He did in the Upper Room, and wash us clean. If He doesn't cleanse us, we cannot go on into the holy place.

Let's talk about this for a moment. When you are born anew, God forgives your sin—that is, your past, present, and future sin. He doesn't just forgive you up to now, for God is outside of now. He made "now" and hung it in a bubble called time. God is all around that bubble as well as in it! So the moment He sees you kneel and ask forgiveness and sees you accept Jesus as your Substitute, He forgives everything in the bubble, everything from this moment on, until the day you burst out of it into the "here" with God.

You may ask, "If all my sin is forgiven at that moment of commitment, why, then, do I need to ask forgiveness once I have found Christ?" The laver of cleansing explains the reason. Fellowship with the Father requires shoes off and clean feet! Your relationship depends on your new birth in Christ, but your fellowship depends on your behavior.

For example, we have two sons. What would happen if one born in our family chose to be a prodigal, left home, and ran away to wallow in a pigsty of his choice? Well, he would always be our son, for our life would be in him; he has been born into our family. His relationship would never change, for it would depend on his birth. But his fellowship with us would depend upon his behavior.

When you've tramped around in a pigsty, and you come to yourself one day and decide to go home and talk to your Father again, then your feet will need cleansing before you can run comfortably around His house. You see, your relationship depends on your birth but your fellowship upon your behavior. Daily you and I trample in dirt somewhere, and we need Jesus to wash our feet. Our head and our hands are still clean, for we are cleansed from the sin principle in our lives by the word He has spoken unto us; but our feet need to be cleaned by repenting daily from sins that have ruined our family fellowship with our heavenly Father.

Now we are in the outer court. Many Christians stop in the outer court of worship. They know what it is to have been to the brazen altar, and they know what it is to say "sorry" prayers and let Jesus keep cleaning them up, but that is all. In fact, the sad thing is that they don't want anything more, or some don't know there is anything more for them to have. They are unaware of a deeper way of walking into the holy place where the priests work and worship. They think the inner holy place is just for the priests or mystics or overenthusiastic new believers! Their worship experience ends up being a pretty shallow and self-centered affair.

THE HOLY PLACE

But you see, we live this side of the cross. The way has been made for all of us to go not only into the holy place but into the holiest of all (Hebrews 10:19). You and I are priests now, for the Bible talks of the priesthood of all believers (1 Peter 2:9). The chief privilege of a priest is access to God, and Jesus made that gloriously possible.

To stay with an experience of a brazen altar and laver of cleansing is not sufficient as far as the One who has graciously come to tabernacle in our midst is concerned. He wants to draw us deeper into worship. He wants to take us to His very heart. There is more of Him that many of us have not yet discovered, and more of us that can involve ourselves in a prayer experience.

As noted before, many believe the holy place is for priests, pastors, nuns—special people like that. During the Exodus days, God set a veil across the entrance to the holy place and holy of holies, and He forbade the people entrance. But now you and I may walk in and enjoy what God has for us of His own presence.

Three pieces of furniture stand in the holy place. First, the candlestick. There was light in the holy place: light to see by, light to serve by, and light to worship by. This represented the illumination from God who "is light [for] in him there is no darkness at all" (1 John 1:5).

As we are drawn nearer to God in our worship experience, He will illuminate that time for us. He will light our way. He has said that His Word will be "a lamp for [our] feet, and a light on [our] path" (Psalm 119:105). Sometimes we need to have light shed on an immediate step. We have arrived at a situation, and we aren't sure which way to handle it. Be reminded that God has promised a light for our feet; He will show us clearly where to step. The Word of God will throw light on the whole situation, and as we read, it will be like a voice behind us saying, "This is the way; walk in it" (Isaiah 30:21).

God also promises light ahead for our path. As we look ahead into our immediate future, the way may look pretty black and foreboding. He is light, and if we are pressing on into a deeper experience of worship or needing insight into a dilemma, we will find light ahead as well as light around us. Even if God calls us to walk through the darkest valley, the valley of the shadow of death, we will find that where there's a shadow, there's always light! God promises we "will never walk in darkness, but will have the light of life" (John 8:12). So as we decide to go deeper, pressing on to know God more, we will meet the light of the golden candlestick and will have His light for our way.

Jesus said, "I am the light of the world" (John 8:12), and then He said, "You are the light of the world" (Matthew 5:14). We are to be like that golden candlestick—bearing high the light for a world that is in darkness. That is how we are to function. The candlestick lit up its entire area, and God intends us not to hide our light, but to let it shine. God promises not only light for our way and light for our world, but light for our worship too.

How can we really worship God? How can we learn how to praise Him aright? Do we just go on saying, "Thank You, Jesus" all our lives? Is this praise? No, not only this. God will throw light on this problem. God will illuminate His Word, and His Spirit will throw light on difficult passages of Scripture. He will enlighten the eyes of our hearts to know what a fantastic thing it is to be invited to enjoy an inheritance in Christ (Ephesians 1:18). He will enlighten our very worship so we shall begin to see God with our inner eyes. The veil will disappear for the Christian who decides to walk in the holy place, and he will begin to see clearly spiritual and heavenly realities.

The presence bread in the holy place consisted of twelve loaves and was sacred food for the priests. Jesus said, "I am the bread of life. Whoever comes to me will never go hungry" (John 6:35). Christians who insist on pressing toward the holiest of all will find the presence bread sustaining them for their priestly duties. God prepared special bread for His priests, and

His choicest fare awaits you in the holy place. As you grow in knowledge of Him, you will find that God will give you fresh bread daily that you may be strong and vigorous as you serve Him and others.

When I first began speaking to groups of people, I worried I would run out of spiritual food for thought. Would I have enough to say? Where would I find fresh material? I have found that as I feast on God, the Presence Bread of life, I have been "strengthened with power through His Spirit in the inner man" (Ephesians 3:16 NASB), and God has always enabled me to speak to and serve those to whom He sent me.

He told me I would fly, but when I couldn't fly anymore I would run; when I couldn't run anymore I would walk, and He told me I would never faint (Isaiah 40:31). Jesus, my Presence Bread, keeps me strong. He sustains and energizes me.

Manna for survival is one thing; bread for the priest is another. Paul wrote that we should grow up to have more mature eating habits. He told us to learn how to be a workman who isn't ashamed to rightly divide the word of truth (2 Timothy 2:15). We are told to grow from collecting enough manna to keep us alive, and learn to feast as priests of the Most High God on the Presence Bread of Christ. Many books, recordings, and helps are available to take us deeper in that holy place. To gather enough for yourself is one thing, but to serve as a priest, you need to gather and feed others too. That sort of appetite is stimulated as you choose to serve God in the holy place.

The priests presented the prayers of the people at the altar of incense. Maybe it is in this very aspect that you can decipher in which area of worship you are living. In the outer court experience, you have learned to get cleaned up. Your prayer life has been mainly self-centered. "I'm dirty, Jesus." "Forgive me, Lord." "Clean me up, Savior." But if you decide to go deeper, you will begin to serve as a priest at the altar of incense. You will present the needs of others before God. You will engage in a ministry of prayer on their behalf. You will begin to know what we were talking about when we discussed Moses, Aaron, and Hur praying for Joshua in the valley.

To live in the light and to be sustained by the Bread of the Presence is to find the desire to pray at that altar. Do you pray more for yourself than for others? Where are you living in the tabernacle?

The holy place is holy. You sense God's presence near. You recognize that you are growing and getting stronger every day. All this is necessary, but friend, even this is not enough. God calls you one step further; He calls you into the holiest of all.

ONE STEP FURTHER

Across this most sacred of all places, where the manifest presence of God was, hung a heavy veil. Only once a year the high priest was allowed to enter in. He carried with him a lamb, perfect and without blemish. A lamb that had been slain as the substitute sacrifice for the whole nation. Entering the holy of holies, the high priest sprinkled the blood of that animal on the mercy seat, which covered the ark wherein lay the righteous demands of a holy God, set within the Law.

When Jesus, the Lamb of God, died on the cross, the veil in the temple across the entrance to the holy of holies was rent in two. A way had been made to the mercy seat for you and for me.

Then Jesus presented Himself to His holy Father as our substitute, and the Father accepted Him on our behalf. Therefore, we may boldly come before "the throne of grace" because of Him (Hebrews 4:16). So don't think the holiest of all is for Aaron, the high priest of the book of Exodus. A way has been made by Jesus, our great High Priest, and He calls us to enter into a worship experience, not just to be enjoyed for a few minutes a year on a religious holiday. He calls us to live there, moment by moment, in the most intimate presence of God.

So let us enter in!

It's time to discover, discuss, and then apply the discoveries you have made. If you are using this for your own study time, record your findings in a notebook.

Summary

In a sentence or two, summarize what this chapter is about.

Discovery

If you are doing this study in a group, split the group into twos and work through the study. Then share the information. If you're working alone, journal about each item.

1. *The tabernacle is the abiding place of God.* In the Old Testament we see the tabernacle as the dwelling place of God—a place where His Shekinah glory marked His presence. In the New

Testament, we find that God has a new dwelling place. Note the progression of the dwelling place of God:

a) Moses: tabernacle of God's glory (Exodus 40:34–35; Numbers 14:10; 16:19; 16:42; 20:6).

b) Solomon: temple of God's greatness (1 Kings 8:11; 2 Chronicles 5:14; 7:1).

c) AD 33: trophies of God's grace (Acts 7:47–50; 17:24; 1 Corinthians 3:16–17; 6:19–20; 2 Corinthians 6:16).

Discussion or Journal

1. The conspicuous presence of God in the Old Testament could be found in a building like the tabernacle or temple. In the New Testament, God is conspicuously present and active in our bodies. What activities should take place in our bodies if they are the activity center of God? (Read 1 Corinthians 6:13, 19–20; 10:31; 12:27; 2 Corinthians 4:10; Romans 6:12; 8:13; Galatians 6:17; Philippians 1:20; James 3:2.)

Decision

1. What in this chapter most applies to you? What do you need to do about it?

2. Make a choice about your worship. Write it down. Do it!

Devotion

1. *The tabernacle was the place of accessibility to God.* In the book of Hebrews, we see Christ contrasted with the Levitical system of sacrifices—the latter portrayed as a shadow of the real thing. What do these verses tell us about such a contrast and the access we now have to God? Take one reference a day for six days: Hebrews 8:1–6; 4:14–16; 9:13–14; 10:19–25; 12:28–29; 13:7–17.

A Personal Spiritual Workout

Each day choose a thought or look up a verse in your notes pertaining to the lessons learned and *meditate* (which means to "chew it over") throughout the day. Pray about it each night.

TWELVE

CALEB AND THE CLOUD

Josiah looked anxiously from his tent toward the center of the camp. He sighed with relief and relaxed, for there it was. Father God knew small boys would find it difficult to get to sleep in the dark in a strange environment, and so He had kindly provided an enormous night-light for His little ones!

Josiah was very small. So many traumatic events had happened in recent days that he could hardly remember his home in Egypt. But the memories he had were horrible. He remembered his mother weeping as she bathed the whiplashes on his father's back—courtesy of the Egyptian taskmasters. He couldn't shut out the horrendous picture of his aunt fighting with the soldiers to avoid his baby cousin being thrown in the Nile. Little wonder Josiah needed a night-light!

Young Josiah remembered the first time he had seen the light. It happened after their escape from Pharaoh. As the angel of death passed over the blood-marked doorposts of the children of Israel, taking to himself the firstborn of Egypt's sons, Josiah watched his nation run away. His father, Caleb, had lifted him in his strong arms to a vantage point on his shoulders, where he could see everything that was happening. Young though he was, little Josiah realized his people were going to be free.

Being in slavery all his life, Josiah could not comprehend the meaning of the word *free*. Maybe it meant no more Pharaoh? It was at that moment, looking back, when he saw something that showed him that being free didn't mean that! Pursuing them furiously were Egypt's best men of war. Josiah could still see the enemy, but the army looked pale and insignificant, and kind of funny, when you looked at them through the fire of the manifest presence of God.

So being free meant peace in the company of the enemy. *God in-between him and me,* Josiah thought. "Is it all right to go to sleep?" he whispered to the warm, fiery light. "Yes, little one," answered Father God. "He that keeps Israel shall neither slumber nor sleep, so there's no point in *both* of us staying awake!" With childlike faith, Josiah believed God, smiled happily, and fell asleep across his father's shoulders.

In the morning the first thing Josiah did was look for the fiery pillar. It was gone. He began looking in all directions for a sight of it and suddenly became aware of people excitedly pointing at a strange shape gliding across the desert at the head of the company. At first Josiah thought the sky had fallen down, but then something about that pillarlike cloud struck him as endearingly familiar, and he knew without anyone telling him that that strange phenomenon was his night-light.

As long as Josiah gazed at it, that calm sense of well-being enveloped him as it had the previous night, and suddenly he knew he never wanted to lose sight of that cloud again. Somehow he realized life could be meaningful only within the radius of its influence.

Being a child, Josiah couldn't articulate words like *radius* and *influence,* but I believe at some point in a childlike way, his little heart reached out toward that cloud and said, "Cloud, I will follow you forever. I will run after you until I can run no more, and I will seek to wholly follow you." Night after night, the pillar of fire lit their way across the desert. Day after day, the cloud determined their schedule and their journey. When the pillar stopped, the children of Israel stopped. When it took off across the desert, whether by day or night, they followed. God was teaching them to be obedient. "In all the travels of the Israelites, whenever the cloud lifted from above the tabernacle, they would set out . . . until the day it lifted. So the cloud of the LORD was over the tabernacle by day, and fire was in the cloud by night, in the sight of all the Israelites during all their travels" (Exodus 40:36–38). The younger we are when we learn to rely on the presence of God to be obedient, the better. To decide to fully follow God is the prerequisite to His fully filling us with the necessary enabling. In other words, the cloud will not fill our earthly tabernacle, as it did that desert structure, unless we have been obedient and are ready to follow further instructions. The writer of Numbers 9:15–23 explains that a decision to be obedient is necessary if the glory of the Lord is to be seen.

THE TENT SORT OF DISAPPEARED

It is interesting to see what happened to the tent in this passage of Scripture: it sort of disappeared! As the people gazed at a structure full of God, they saw a dim shape of the earthly tabernacle, but the glory filled their vision. The writer stated, "so it was continuously" (v. 16 NASB).

When Paul, writing to the Ephesians, commanded them to be "filled with the Spirit" (Ephesians 5:18), he was saying, "So it can be continuously." A decision to wholly follow the Lord in obedience will result in a definite sense of the presence of God about you. People will dimly see your "tabernacle" but will catch a glimpse of the glory of the Lord. This can be a continual thing. But keep in mind that if the people were to enjoy the glory of the Lord, they had to endure following the cloud. We want the blessings of the promised land without conditions. "Isn't it all of grace?" we ask. "Can't we expect God to give us presents without any conditions?" The answer to that is, "No. There is no blessing without obedience!" It's not easy, but then God never promised us that following Him would be a piece of cake!

If you think about it, following that cloud must not have been easy for all of those families. Sometimes it couldn't have been very convenient. Can you imagine being Josiah's mother, getting all the children to sleep after a day's hard trek through the desert, and suddenly that unpredictable cloud takes off again? "Oh no," she must have said. "Not now, not again!" It must have been very tempting to just stay put and rest awhile, hoping to catch up later. But then she ran the risk of not ever being able to catch up again!

That is our problem too. We might not catch up again if we lose sight of the glory of the Lord. We may lose our sense of direction and wander aimlessly around until we die. That cloud was most unpredictable, but one thing we do know: Caleb's family was obedient, and that little boy learned to ask, "When?" and not to ask, "Why?"

THE BLESSING OF THE CHILDREN LAY IN THE OBEDIENCE OF THE PARENTS

When the glory of the Lord is the motivating factor in parents' lives, their children will have the best chance in the world of entering into the blessings of the promised land. God is glorified when the cloud fills the tent and when His people wholly obey.

Our own children have told us there was an impact on their lives when we immigrated to the United States, leaving our beloved England behind. It was hard. My husband and I left behind two widowed mothers, but they watched us be obedient to the leading of the Lord and they participated in this step of faith too.

I remember sitting in a bedroom in England on the way to join my husband in South Africa. Our three children were scattered around the world, and I felt pretty lonely and homesick for them. I began to ask myself whatever was I doing leaving them. Surely they would be affected! I read this passage and realized that they would be affected if I followed the cloud to South Africa, but they would be affected only for good! Like Josiah's parents, I must insist on the glory of the Lord being my priority. In my obedience lay the hope of their blessing. And so indeed it turned out to be. That period was a marvelous experience for them of growth in God. Now all three of our kids are in ministry themselves—a testimony to the principle that the blessing of the children lies in the obedience of the parents!

Josiah was certainly blessed by his parents' obedience, as were our three teenagers.

Yet we read in Exodus that not all parents were obedient. Too many grumbled and groused, and their rebellious attitude was not lost on the children. Remember the G virus? Griping was contagious, and many of the children died on the way, as well as their parents. But God blessed Caleb's family for their commitment. What a testimony God gave to Caleb! "But because my servant Caleb has a different spirit and follows me wholeheartedly, I will bring him into the land he went to, and his descendants will inherit it" (Numbers 14:24).

CALEB, SERVANT OF GOD

The first thing God said about Caleb was that Caleb was His *servant.* The joys of personal victory are wrapped up in the joys of personal service. Don't forget that serving God doesn't only mean priestly tabernacle service. It involves your gifts and abilities—in fact, all you are as a person—serving your people.

Numbers 13:1–6 states that Caleb had become a ruler of his tribe. He was one of the leaders of Israel. This involved self-sacrificing service. He was asked to hazard his life on a spy mission into Canaan, and he gladly set out on behalf of others to investigate the promised land. If God privileges us with the responsibilities of leadership, those responsibilities must inevitably involve self-sacrifice on behalf of others. If God were to tell Moses to write down something about you, would he write, "He is My servant"? Are you hazarding your life for people—giving your life away?

God says something else about Caleb. Having talked about his servanthood, God goes on to comment on his spirit. Caleb's attitude contrasted with the grumbling, mumbling, disobedient spirit of the other leadership, and God commended him for it (Numbers 14:22–24). Caleb didn't catch the G virus! He kept himself clean and healthy spiritually and refused to criticize his leaders.

SERVING OUR PEOPLE AND FIGHTING OUR GIANTS

We think of David as the great giant killer, but Caleb killed a whole mountain full of giants! I believe God loves a daring disciple: a Daniel who will brave the lions' den, a David who will laugh in a giant's face, and a Peter who will leap out of his boat (even if he rocks it). Joshua 14:6–15 is a marvelous passage of the Bible that shows us this vibrant faith-filled spirit of Caleb.

Moses was dead, and the children of the children of Israel were in the promised land. Now it was time to possess their possessions. Caleb came to Joshua and reminded him he was forty years of age when Moses sent him to explore the land. Moses had promised Caleb the land on which his feet had walked as an inheritance as a reward for his faith and obedience. He was now eighty-five years of age. "I am still as strong today as the day Moses sent me out; I am just as vigorous to go out to battle now as I was then. Now give me this hill country that the LORD promised me that day," he commanded Joshua (Joshua 14:11–12). The King James Version says, "Give me this mountain." I love that!

I love the sheer audacity that Caleb showed at this time in his life. It's not every man who will take on a mountain full of giants at the ripe old age of eighty-five! Caleb's obedient spirit had sustained him, and he wasn't finished yet! Only in the Christian life can you expect a servant and a soldier all rolled up in one. We must serve our people and we must fight our giants. Some of us have a mountain full of giants facing us. Unlike Caleb, we may choose some other activity for our years of retirement. This story is laced with old-timers! Moses, Miriam, and Aaron were probably well into their nineties or more at this point in the story.

A committed follower will tackle the highest mountain, infested with the nastiest giants, with a strong spirit of faith in God, who he or she believes is as big and powerful as His promises. His prayer request will be, "Give me this mountain," not, "Make this mountain disappear from sight." Listen to Caleb: "If the LORD is with me, I will drive them out of the land, just as the LORD said" (v. 12 NLT).

Even in the promised land, living a Christian life that is really working, we will still encounter mountains and giants. But Caleb's cloud covered his life, and he was filled full through following God. He could say, "He is able; therefore I am able." Check the contrast of unbelieving talk in Numbers 13:31. "We are not able!" said the rest of the spies in their report to Moses (NKJV). Faith doesn't only believe God can; faith believes God will. This was the spirit that God commended in Caleb, His servant.

What is the language of your heart? What huge problem is looking at you? Are you saying, "He is able," or are you saying, "He is not"? How big is your faith? Learn to look at your problems through the cloud, and don't look at the cloud through the problems!

GOD'S BLESSING ON THE CHILDREN

The last thing God had to say about Caleb was a word concerning his children. God promised blessing to his children: they would possess the land. What do I want for my children? What do you want for yours? I want the blessing of God promised to Caleb. I want nothing less than the glory-cloud experience for them. I want them to grow up saying, "Give me this mountain," and then don the armor of the Lord and fight through to victory. I want God to be able to commend my children for their servanthood and their spirit. That's what I want, and I can see from this passage that all that will probably be caught, not taught, as they see me doggedly pursuing the cloud. Yes, I have a part to play. My job is to be faithful.

Will you go in, not for your own sake only, but for your children's sake as well? Why don't you possess your possessions? Do I hear you say, as the unbelieving elders did, "But the people are strong, the cities are walled, and the giants are ready to gobble us up," or will you say with Caleb, "Let us go up at once . . . for we are well able to overcome"?

As I travel this world at the young age of eighty-two, I am faced with giants on a daily basis. There are the giants of discouragement, jet lag, and exhaustion. There are the giants of worry, fear, and depression. Then there are the mountains of sorrow, poverty, and persecution, and the sheer evil seen everywhere, often looking so big and so powerful it is overwhelming.

But listen to me! The fire and the cloud lead me, the Lord fights for me, and His precious promises are coming true each and every day of my life! How good of God to let me live long enough to see Him prove Himself so strong on my behalf.

Laugh with me, so I can laugh at all those giants who threaten me. So I can say with absolute confidence and a great shout of faith, "Let us go up at once—because the Lord is on my side!"

It's time to discover, discuss, and then apply the discoveries you have made. If you are using this for your own study time, record your findings in a notebook.

Summary

In a sentence or two, summarize what this chapter is about.

Discovery

1. Read Numbers 13:26–33 and answer the following questions:
   a) What sort of spy are you?
   b) Name some of the giants (things that are bigger than you) that you face.
   c) What is the end result of being a bad spy (Numbers 14:1)?

Discussion or Journal

1. Read Numbers 14:20–38 and respond to the following:
   a) How many chances did God give the people (vv. 22, 27)?
   b) Note God's care for His children (v. 31).
   c) Note the blessings of obedience (vv. 36–38).

Decision

1. Will you follow the cloud?
2. What is the Lord asking you to be obedient about?

Devotion

1. Read Joshua 14:6–15.
   a) Pray about the strength you need for your particular war.
   b) Try to pray as Caleb did, "Give me this mountain!"
   c) Make a list of all the characteristics of Caleb. Pray about them for yourself, your family, your church, and your world.

A Personal Spiritual Workout

Each day choose a thought or look up a verse in your notes pertaining to the lessons learned and *meditate* (which means to "chew it over") throughout the day. Pray about it each night.

NOTES

Chapter 1: A Moses Moment
1. Kim Hubbard, "Gloria Considers Gloria," *People Weekly* (New York), 37:3 (January 27, 1992), 46.
2. "Now I Belong to Jesus," copyright ©1938, 1943 Norman J. Clayton. Renewed 1966, 1971 Wordspring Music, Inc. (Admin. by Word Music Group, Inc.)

Chapter 2: Palace Training
1. Richard Foster, *Celebration of Discipline,* 20th anniversary ed. (New York: HarperCollins, 1998), 81, 93.

Chapter 5: The Other Side of Redemption
1. Edward Mote, "My Hope is Built on Nothing Less," 1834.
2. Go to www.justbetweenus.org for more information on *Just Between Us.*
3. C. I. Scofield, *The Scofield Reference Bible* (New York: Oxford University Press, 1945), 89.

Chapter 6: Manna in the Morning
1. Quotes in this paragraph are the author's paraphrase from Exodus 16.

Chapter 7: Rock of Ages

1. Augustus Toplady, "Rock of Ages, Cleft for Me," 1776.
2. Ruth Paxson, *Life on the Highest Plane*, reprint (Grand Rapids, MI: Kregel Publications, 1996), 206–8.

Chapter 8: The Schoolmaster

1. C. S. Lewis, *Mere Christianity*, reprint (New York: HarperOne, 2001), 137.
2. Quotes in this paragraph are the author's paraphrase from Exodus 19.

ABOUT THE AUTHOR

JILL BRISCOE was born in Liverpool, England, in 1935. Educated at Cambridge, she taught school for a number of years before marrying Stuart and raising their three children. In addition to sharing with her husband in ministry with Torchbearers and in pastoring a church in the United States for thirty years, Jill has written more than forty books, traveled on every continent teaching and encouraging, served on the boards of Christianity Today and World Relief, and now acts as executive editor of the magazine for women called *Just Between Us*. Jill can be heard regularly on the worldwide media ministry *Telling the Truth*. She is proud to be called "Nana" by thirteen grandchildren.